I'VE been making quilts since 1981, and a few years ago the organiser of The National Quilt Championships asked me to demonstrate at a quilt show. Imagine my horror when I saw the advertisement, which told the quilters attending that they could 'Meet the experts.' A few years on I've found that other quilters just love it when I mention that I make lots of mistakes and explain how I cover them up.

Life's too short to be very pernickety about every seam being completely straight and every join perfect. I don't intend to be so slapdash: it just happens! When all is said and done it's meant to be fun; if it all becomes a chore we might as well take up a less creative hobby like stamp-collecting ...

Maybe you're a perfect quilter who never makes mistakes: all your quilts hang as straight as a die, and you don't have problems with wonky bottoms (on your quilts or yourself!) You have gourmet meals ready dead on 7 every night, you have a lithe figure, and short-cuts and fudging aren't in your vocabulary. If so, this book isn't for you!

If on the other hand you are, like me, a bodger, in this book I'll tell you how to fudge

and bodge with alacrity and a smile. No-one will ever know that those charming little touches are covering up some quilting disasters – unless you're a big-mouth like me and you go and tell the whole world. I try and make each of my quilting calamities into a feature, so that it seems as if the final effect was intended all along. A friend of mine says 'They aren't mistakes; they're opportunities'; I think that's a really good philosophy to keep us cheerful and sane. So sit back, relax, make yourself a cup of coffee, and enjoy.

BEAUTIFUL BODGES

In life, as well as in quilting, difficulties and disasters can be made into opportunities with a bit of lateral, creative thinking. My whole life has been tinged with disasters which have, in retrospect, changed my life for the better. My mother died of cancer when I was 17; obviously this was devastating, but it actually made me very self-reliant. I had to learn to cook and housekeep for my father, and I was able to try out my culinary disasters on him rather than on my future husband.

18 months later my father re-married; a charming lady who then turned into the storybook 'wicked stepmother.' I left home and lived in a bed-sit. John (my then boyfriend and now long-suffering husband of 37 years) had also been abandoned! His family decided to move hundreds of miles away, so he was also in a bed-sit. In those days one didn't join forces unless married, so we married at a very young age and luckily have survived; I think that not having family to run back to was an advantage. These early difficult experiences have made me a very cheerful person, as I remember the sad times and know how lucky I am.

So, if you suddenly make a dreadful mistake on one of your quilts, don't assume that all is lost! This could be just the creative opportunity you've been looking for, to add that special touch to your quilt. In this section I'll show you all kinds of ways to turn your little 'accidents' into features. I looked up the word 'bodge' in the dictionary: *Bodge: same as botch, a clumsy patch. Bodger: an old name for travelling pedlars who turned beechwood to make chairs legs. A clumsy worker.* I'm using it in the sense of making mistakes and ingeniously trying to cover them up. Some people say 'fudging.' Dictionary definition: *Fudge: an inserted patch in a newspaper, to fudge: to cheat, to fail, to dodge, to obscure or cover up.* But I always think of fudge as a deliciously naughty sweet.

I actually call one of my talks *Beautiful Bodges*, which has caused some problems. I was once introduced thus: 'Dorothy Stapleton will now talk to us on beautiful bodies.' Much amazement from the audience, who thought they were attending a patchwork talk (also, seeing me, they were probably thinking 'She wants to take her own advice ...') This was corrected by someone to 'bodges,' then someone else misheard and said 'Why is she talking about badgers?' When they put up notices in a local needlecraft shop advertising the talk, the assistant said 'I haven't heard of bodging – is it a new technical term?' It certainly is in my book!

Left: buttons on Who Would Marry a Quilter?
Below: this detail of Sartorial Elegance features buttons, machine quilting and labels covering clumsy joins!

Above: if you're not good at joining blocks, try putting spaces between them as I've done on They Must be Useful for Something. Below: I'm Only a Mum; the balls are stuffed to avoid puckering

Stuff it!

If your appliqué shapes are causing you trouble, don't go through all the hassle of unpicking them: it's amazing what a little stuffing will do to even out the problem.

Wonky sides and wobbly bottoms

are a problem for many of us, but here I'm talking about your quilts! On these pages you'll find first aid for that quilt that just won't hang straight – and ways to disguise dodgy edges, too.

Covering up those machine-quilting booboos

Machine-quilting isn't always as easy as it looks: here are some ways to disguise the mistakes when the pattern doesn't go quite right!

Stains and other pains

Take-away curry on your sofa throw? Can't get the pencil marks off your current patchwork project? Don't panic: help is at hand, with these simple remedies for common stains and marks.

Buttons and beads

are wonderful for covering bodges and adding texture and visual interest to your quilts. If you can't make the corners of your blocks match, or have a few lumps and bumps in your quilt, try some of these ideas.

Stuff it!

Stuffing from the back, or trapunto as it's properly called, is a very useful tool for saving some disasters. I've found that sometimes with appliqué everything lies perfectly flat and looks super, then when it's quilted it seems to pucker and appear wrinkled up. Never fear: a bit of stuffing works wonders.

Make a small hole in the back of the work and poke in teased-out wadding with a knitting needle or blunt bodkin. The only difficulty then is how to disguise the holes. If, for instance you have a circle, as I had for the babies' faces in *Baby Talk* (see page 52, and detail on page 6), you could copy the method I used on that piece. I made a small slit at each side of the face on the back of the quilt and stuffed the shapes with wadding; I then oversewed the edges of the slits together, and as they were next to the quilted line they didn't show.

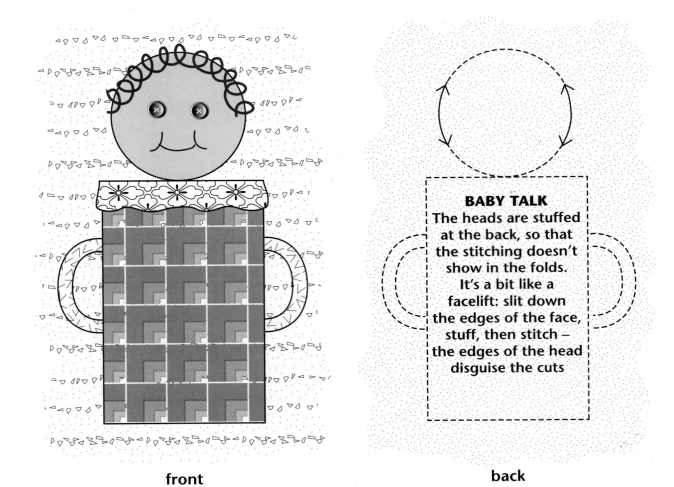

BABY TALK
The heads are stuffed at the back, so that the stitching doesn't show in the folds. It's a bit like a facelift: slit down the edges of the face, stuff, then stitch – the edges of the head disguise the cuts

front   back

The alternative is to make a feature of the join and embellish it with embroidery stitches. In my quilt *I'm Only a Mum* (see page 3), made in 1997, I stuffed all the different balls the woman is juggling in the air. As they were quite large and the back was fairly pale, I covered the overcast join with some feather stitch to make it look intended. If you have a backing fabric which is dark-coloured and a very 'busy' pattern, the joins will hardly show.

I included a photograph of this quilt in my previous book but didn't explain it. I sometimes get an idea for a quilt from a passing remark. My daughter-in-law said that when she went to parties and people asked what her job was, she was embarrassed to say 'I'm only a Mum.' I said, 'It's the most important job in the world, and the versatility required is amazing.' So this quilt is a Mum wearing all the hats that are required: a mortar board, a nurse's hat, a woolly hat and a halo! She is juggling all the impossible questions small children constantly ask, usually as you're trying to concentrate on something else. Each ball has two questions, which are:

Why isn't tea ready?	*Why do birds have white poos?*
What is 9468 x 3½?	*What does **** mean?*
Who is God's daddy?	*Who is taking me to cubs?*
Where do babies come from?	*Where is Timbuktu?*
When will we be there?	*When will my tummy feel better?*

My son had friends who built their own yacht and then set sail for New Zealand: they warned their two small boys that the only rule there would be on the voyage was that nobody was to say 'When will we be there?'!

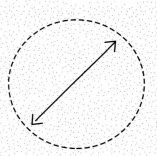
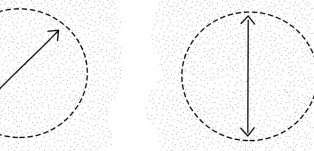

I'M ONLY A MUM
I slit the backs of the circles either diagonally or straight (above), stuffed them, then re-stitched in either herringbone or feather stitch (below)

front

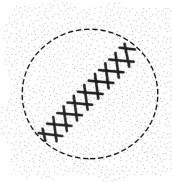
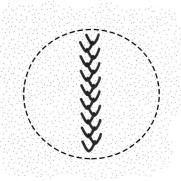

back

Above: I stuffed the head of each baby in Baby Talk, *to even out the surface*

For my quilt *What Is?* I decided to make it reversible, and the large question mark motifs were stitched in place front and back before I realised that they were going to have to be stuffed, as they were all puckered up. So I made the holes for the stuffing on the front of the quilt in two or three places, poked in fluffed-up wadding with a knitting needle, then covered the evidence with a lazy daisy stitch, thus making a feature out of the mistake. I added more flowers at the corner of each block as the edges were slightly out of alignment and this detail takes the eye away from the mistakes.

On What is … ?, *the shapes were already outlined with fancy stitches, so I made holes, stuffed the shapes and then covered each slit with an embroidered flower (above and right). Each flower was created from lazy daisy (detached chain) stitches, with several French knots in the centre. More embroidered flowers covered up wonky corners on the blocks!*

Wonky sides and wobbly bottoms

Yes, I'm sure we can all identify with this, but I'm actually referring to quilts, not people ... I find it a recurring problem to get the sides and bottoms of my quilts straight, or even looking remotely straight.

If you're making a bed quilt you'll probably find that no one will even notice if the sides or bottom aren't completely true. I made a medallion quilt for our silver wedding many years ago: had it on the bed for years, and it looked just fine. Then it was hung in an exhibition and suddenly appeared to be very wonky; at this stage I suddenly realised that I'd left one whole row of the pattern out! As it's for my bed and it doesn't show, I really don't mind; and as the Persian carpet-makers say: 'Always have a deliberate mistake as only Allah is perfect.' I think this quilt might have taken the premise to extremes though.

The real horror in this category was my quilt *Mediterranean Sunset* (left). It's fairly large (49x69in, 125x175cm), and is made of 247 blocks of one-inch-strip log cabin. It also has a heavily hand-quilted border. As you know, log cabin can get progressively out of hand and become more and more wonky – and the smaller the strips, the worse the problem. I will solve this problem for you on page 29, but at the time I made this quilt I hadn't learnt the easy method. It was accepted for the Quilters' Guild 5th Exhibition at Edinburgh Art Gallery; when I finished it and proudly hung it up, it was a disaster; the side was so crooked that John helpfully suggested I took a tuck in it. I was nearly in tears: all that work for nothing.

I decided to stretch the quilt as if it were a tapestry or embroidery. I dampened it all over by spraying it with a squeezy water bottle (used for dampening the ironing); I then pinned it to the spare bedroom carpet with dressmaking pins, starting at the top and pulling it taut. I left it for three or four days till it was dry and stretched, and, relief: it

Try these ideas for decorative hems

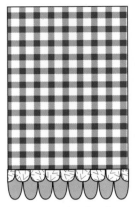

double row of scallop shapes

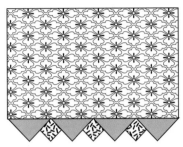

double row of prairie points

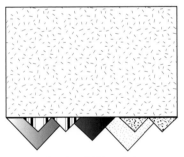

triangles of different sizes

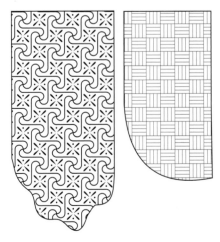

asymmetric bottom edges

hung straight. I went to the exhibition in fear and trembling in case it had reverted to its former wobbles, but luckily it hadn't. I think that part of my problem is not putting the bindings on correctly. (In case you find that this is your problem, check out the correct way in the *Basic Boring Bits* at the back of the book.)

An alternative solution is to make the sides and bottom deliberately uneven. There are many more uneven-shaped quilts around these days; maybe I'm not the only one with this recurring problem. I have used this technique in *They Must be Useful for Something* (opposite top), made in 2000. I had been sun printing as described on page 35, and was madly trying to print anything and everything I could lay my hands on. I found that the mesh bags which are supplied for washing tablets printed a treat; each time you buy a box of tablets they give you another mesh bag with a blue toggle to pull it tight, and I'd been saving them thinking that they must have some use.

I made the quilt using the envelope method (see page 40), but deliberately left the sides and bottom uneven; as in this method of construction each panel is neatly turned, it doesn't present a fraying problem. I hand-stitched the sides of all the blocks with buttonhole stitch just to add more interest. The bottom and some edges have the blue toggles hanging from the hems as if they were a fringe. I then thought of ridiculous uses for them in appliquéd picture panels: a trawl net, a hairnet, a beekeeper's hat, a saucy bikini and a Dorothy bag.

I've never known why little drawstring bags are known as Dorothy bags. I've always hated the name Dorothy; it's most people's granny's name. I usually get the full name, although I have been known in my time as Dot, Dotty, Doffy – and my grandchildren call me Doro. I did a lot of family history research and the earliest person I traced back was a Dorothy Brearley in 1775; this was my maiden name, so I began to learn to like it more.

I was sewing some of the blocks for this piece at a quilting show and was amazed how many women said that they also had been saving the bags hoping to find a use for them. Some suggestions were:

- Putting bulbs from patio pots in them and burying them in the ground over the summer. By leaving the blue toggle above ground they can easily be found again for re-planting in the winter.

- Putting small socks or tights in them to stop tangling in the washing machine.

- Putting strips for log cabin inside separate bags, sorted by colour; they can then be hung on hooks or from pins on a pinboard.

- Keeping receipts for items that might need to be returned to a shop at a later date.

So the moral of this tale is: you make a silly quilt and get some very sensible ideas from other quilters.

Fragments from the Sun (see page 36, and detail opposite below) is another example of a quilt which ended up with an asymmetric hemline. It's a blue-printed quilt (see page 35) which I'd entered for The National Quilt Championships before it was finished; I intended it to be a traditional-shaped oblong wall quilt. As I worked on it, though, I realised it was looking rather strange the way round I'd intended it (landscape format).

Asymmetric quilt designs can be very effective; try finishing the bottom off with tassels

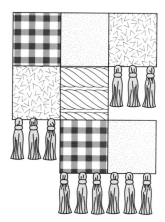

TIP

When I showed They Must be Useful for Something *at a talk, one woman said 'You've answered a question that's been bothering me.' She's a junior-school maths teacher, and had noticed that other teachers had nice little mesh bags to keep counters in. She'd tried to find them in the educational catalogue without success!*

Right: the different blocks in They Must be Useful for Something *were created separately then joined in an asymmetric design*

Below: detail of Fragments from the Sun, *showing the asymmetric hem*

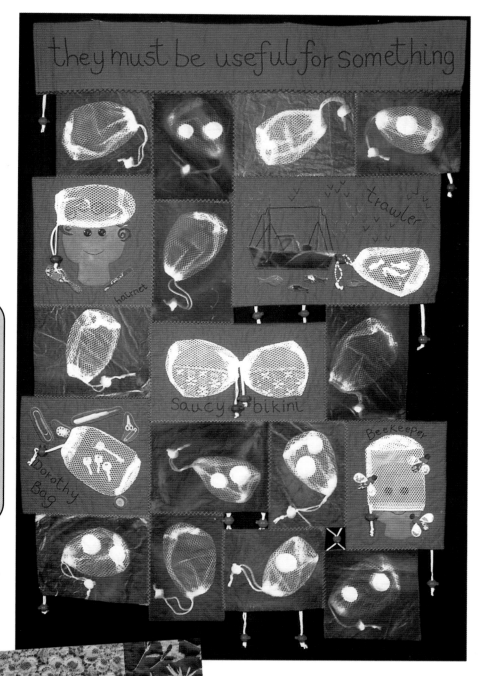

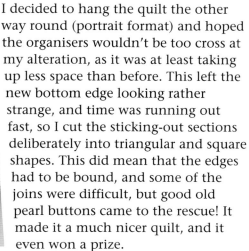

I decided to hang the quilt the other way round (portrait format) and hoped the organisers wouldn't be too cross at my alteration, as it was at least taking up less space than before. This left the new bottom edge looking rather strange, and time was running out fast, so I cut the sticking-out sections deliberately into triangular and square shapes. This did mean that the edges had to be bound, and some of the joins were difficult, but good old pearl buttons came to the rescue! It made it a much nicer quilt, and it even won a prize.

Ways to **force** your quilt to hang straight

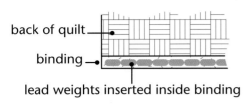

back of quilt
binding
lead weights inserted inside binding

Curtain weights

I find curtain weights invaluable for this purpose; you can buy them either in the form of little lead discs, used for the hems of expensive curtains, or a continuous strip of lead beads held in a strip of cotton. Both types are available from curtain shops. This sounds a rather drastic solution, but the strip is sewn between the layers of the bottom binding and is therefore invisible. The only snag of the extra weight is if you're sending your quilt through the post, as the added weight incurs extra costs!

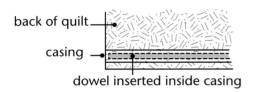

back of quilt
casing
dowel inserted inside casing

A wooden rod

Make a channel at the bottom of the quilt as you would for the top (see *Basic Boring Bits*) and insert a wooden dowel or rod. (This can be a much smaller channel – say an inch wide.) I rather think this would be frowned upon in an exhibition, but if the quilt is hanging in the house and each time you walk by it you think 'I wish I'd made that bottom hang straight,' it's a simple and easy solution.

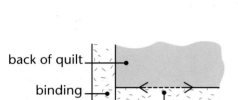

back of quilt
binding
small slits cut in back seam of binding

Padding

This can save a wonky side and a wobbly bottom a treat. It's the same principle as wearing an all-enveloping anorak! I used this technique in desperation on *I Hate Housework*; this quilt, you'll remember, was made entirely out of washing and dish cloths (detail below). I made a two-inch border and used yellow table napkins and 1930s kitchen curtaining from a jumble sale. Joining the two different-weave fabrics made them pull and pucker: it looked dreadful. The exhibition I was making it for was looming, so I made small holes in the back seam of the binding and inserted teased-out wadding, poking it in using a narrow ruler. I then added a one-inch strip of fabric to cover the holes, and herringbone-stitched over the lot to make a feature of it.

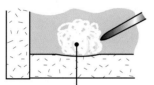

small amounts of wadding pushed into the binding

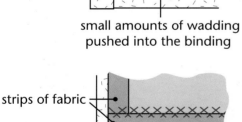

strips of fabric
lines of herringbone stitch

TIP

To get an idea of how a finished quilt will look, and to check the balance of the shapes and colours, use a door spy (available from hardware shops). When you look through it, everything appears distant and the balance – or lack of it – will show up. Another tip is to look at the quilt in a mirror.

Covering up those machine-quilting booboos

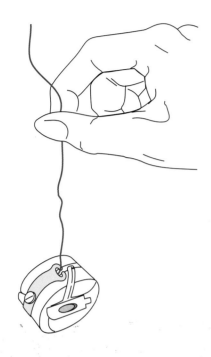

Most quilters eventually realise that they simply can't hand quilt every project because of time pressures, and many quilters find that they get strains and pains in their arms and hands through too much hand quilting. When this happens, machine quilting becomes the preferred method – and some people just prefer quilting by machine. I find, though, that however fine the quilting appears on the top of the work, when you turn it over there can be horrible puckers on the back. What can be done to solve this?

If you have a patterned back to your quilt it will hide a multitude of sins, and you can get away with using the same thread in the bobbin as the top thread. This can make the top look better and the tension appear more even. This is one reason why I like making my quilts using the envelope method, as then you're only quilting small portions at one time, and if one portion is really disastrous it can be replaced.

If you invest in an extra bobbin case for your machine and alter the tension to make it suitable for machine quilting (see left), this is a great help; it saves all that messing about with a screwdriver each time you change from quilting to straight sewing.

There are, however, times on a large quilt when suddenly you realise there's no way out: the quilting is puckered up and it's near the middle. Short of abandoning the whole thing, a bodge has to be effected. In *Who Would Marry a Quilter?* this happened (see photo on page 13). I made the quilt far bigger than I intended by cutting out the husband's head too large. The quilt therefore got larger, and more and more unwieldy. The final quilt measures 58x78in!

I then thought I would disguise these nasty bits by appliquéing something on top. I hit on the idea of cotton reel shapes, so added them on two areas. They made the quilt look much more interesting, so I added more, and then came up with the idea of having the unravelled one spelling out 'Who would marry a quilter?' So once again the mistake helped create a much better quilt than the one I originally intended. This won a second prize at the NPC and was chosen to be in an exhibition in the USA, so obviously it didn't detract from the quilt.

I study husbands when I'm demonstrating at shows; some are very interested in the quilts and come and ask questions, but some really do look very sad. How happy would you look at a model railway exhibition? The idea of this quilt is the poor man is sitting in an over-the-top quilter's house. Everything is quilted or patched: the pictures on the walls, the tea-cosy – even the mug has 'I love quilting' on it.

The absent wife's calendar is on the wall with her week's appointments:

MONDAY:	Me out quilt group
TUESDAY:	Me out committee meeting
WEDNESDAY:	Sewing evening here

TIP

To adjust your bobbin, let the bobbin case hang by the thread. First of all it should just hang there, but if you jerk your hand upwards as if working a yoyo, the bobbin case should fall gently. If it falls really easily, the tension is too loose; if it won't budge, the tension is too tight. Adjust the little screw on the side of the bobbin case very slightly to tighten or slacken the tension.

Buy a second bobbin case and adjust it for machine quilting, then you've always got one ready. Mark this case with a little blob of nail varnish.

THURSDAY:	Area day 10-4
FRIDAY:	Set up exhibition
SATURDAY:	Quilt exhibition
SUNDAY:	My mother to lunch

The tablecloth is edged in old lace from my grandmother's collection. (I didn't cut up a piece of good lace: it did have holes in it and was an edge piece, probably intended for a tablecloth or bedspread.) The husband's jacket has some buttons falling off, and some sewn on with the wrong-coloured thread; his tie is a 'real' tie covered in cotton threads, as is the jacket. (This was quite a problem: to make it look frayed and tatty without it looking like shoddy work.) There's a note left on the table: 'Darling, see you later, tea in fridge.' The cotton reels are scattered around (see detail below), with the final one spelling out the title.

The pictures on the wall are leftovers from other projects. I never throw anything out on the premise that it will come in useful sometime, and it usually does. I tried to make the husband look very unlike John, my husband, as the poor thing does have to put up with a lot without everyone pointing at him in recognition. Many quilters have said about the man on the quilt: 'He doesn't look like your husband, but he does look like mine!'

Right: Who Would Marry a Quilter*? Below: detail*

I used a cotton reel shape (top) on Who Would Marry a Quilter?*; the other shapes here would also work well to cover a multitude of quilting sins!*

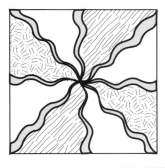

Appliqué shapes on blocks

You can use this technique for any type of quilt; there's a current vogue for adding appliqué on top of traditional blocks. Could it be that the appliquéd patches are covering up some bodgy work? Maybe the fabric ran as it hadn't been pre-washed (see page 14) ... For embellishment or for covering mistakes, try some of the designs on the left. (If you're not sure your appliqué is up to scratch, try the quick and easy methods on pages 25-28.)

Stains and other pains

You spend ages making a quilt, then when it's nearly finished you prick your finger or spill your tea on it: total disaster. Not necessarily: there are lots of tried and tested ways of removing stains.

There are also certain precautions you can take. Never trust any fabric to be entirely colour-fast, even if you were assured in the shop that it is. I always wash any newly-acquired fabric immediately before it's stashed away for future use. I know it's a pain, as it looks so pristine and nicely stiffened. To restore that appearance you can spray-starch it as you iron it after washing; do this before stashing it away – the starch makes it easier to cut and mark, and works a treat with floppy fabrics such as lawns. I was once given five sacks of unwanted rag-bag fabrics and, as it all appeared to be old clothes and scraps from dressmaking, didn't wash the contents. Big mistake: it turned out that the donor had been trying out dyeing, without much success, and all the red fabrics ran onto my cream calico. It really wouldn't come out – but you could use the ideas on pages 11-13 to disguise such disasters.

One stain removal product still fills me with dread: *carbontetrachloride* (what a name). It's basically lighter fuel. I used to teach small boys art in a prep school; they kept on getting the Copydex glue on their clothes, much to their mothers' annoyance, so I sent for some removing fluid which turned out to be the dreaded carbontetrachloride. A year later, when my first son was a baby, I was minding my niece and nephew – aged 2 and 4 – while my sister had another baby. My son got tar on his little white kid shoes, so while I was running their evening bath I got out the dreaded bottle of stain remover. It got the tar off, but I left the container on the side of the bath; that was the first day Paul decided he could pull himself up onto his feet, and he grabbed the bottle and drank it.

We didn't have a telephone, and John was out in the car, so the neighbours took Paul and me to the hospital where they pumped his stomach. He had to stay in hospital for five days to check that it hadn't affected his lungs. My brother-in-law and other sister came to collect the two children, but their car broke down on the way; they were towed to our house by the rescue services. Eventually Paul and I were discharged from hospital and I realised I had forgotten the baby seat for the car (it was in the 1960s when seat belts hadn't been invented); so I had to ask the hospital to lend me some bandages to tie him to the front seat. You can understand now my antipathy to carbontetrachloride! So, the moral is: do be careful with cleaning products.

I find that with bed quilts which are washable, the best solution for most spillages is to soak them in the bath immediately, then wash either in biological washing powder or Vanish soap.

I can vouch for this as the Dresden Plate – mostly calico – wedding quilt I made for my son (same one as above: he really is accident prone!) suffered a disaster. They were eating curry in bed and spilt some. Luckily my daughter-in-law rang and said 'Help!', and it all came off as above.

For specific stains, the box below is a guide to things which might help to clear them up. A good idea is to try and reproduce the stain on a similar piece of fabric then try different things to remove it; eg, if the problem is chewing gum on a cotton quilt, stick some to a piece of cotton fabric then try out the remedy to see if it works. If so, use the same technique on the real stain. If not, try something else!

A quick guide to stain removal

Adhesives and sticky tape
methylated spirit

Ball-point pen
acetone (nail varnish remover), then soapy water

Beer
soak in biological washing powder

Blood
use salt in cold water, or spit on a cloth and rub

old stubborn stains: 1tsp hydrogen peroxide in 8tbsp water; sponge

Chocolate
Sponge with cool soapy water; sprinkle with borax and leave half an hour, then rinse

Coffee or tea
rinse and soak overnight in biological washing powder; sponge with borax solution

Contact adhesive
acetone (nail varnish remover)

Crayon
dab with methylated spirit, then wash in detergent.

Felt-tip pen
as for ball-point pen

Fruit juices
rinse and wash as for coffee and tea

Lipstick
proprietary make-up stain remover

Mildew
one part hydrogen peroxide to six parts water

Pencil
roll some white bread in your fingers till soggy, then use it to erase the mark (some quilt shops sell an eraser for removing pencil marks from fabric)

Scorch marks
dab with mixture of soapy water and 1tsp borax

Spirits
wash in cold water

Tar
eucalyptus oil (not as my experience!)

Urine and vomit (for baby quilts)
wash in biological powder

Wine, red
mop up, then blot with white wine; rinse in water

Or cover with a thick layer of table salt to soak up the colour; when the salt is dry, wash as usual

Wine, white
rinse in warm water; sponge with borax solution

You can buy special stain-removing products in hardware shops, but usually these disasters happen in the evening when the shops are shut!

It's ironic that I had just typed this section and went to visit my son, who has a walnut tree in his garden. We picked the nuts off the ground eagerly and I prised the green outer shells open with my fingernails. I realised that my hands were rather brown but thought it would wash off; no such luck – it's an indelible dye. We were due at a ruby wedding party the next day. I tried bleach, lemon juice, tar remover, all to no avail; I even did lots of clothes washing by hand! I was very embarrassed at the party, looking like an off-duty garage mechanic. So I deduce that walnut is a stain with no antidote. It wore off after a week ...

Buttons and beads

Buttons are a godsend: I use them frequently in my quilts. You can buy badges which carry the slogan 'Quilters don't sew buttons,' and I'm probably as bad as most quilters at lovingly and carefully attaching a decorative button onto a quilt while using a safety pin on my cuff to avoid sewing on the button that's gone AWOL. Beads, too, are wonderful 'little helpers' for quilters.

The reason that buttons are so useful is that they can cover up that bad join. You know the problem: pin the seam, check that it really meets, make sure one seam is facing to the left and the other to the right to get a really sharp flat join. Then machine it, open it out, and disaster: it's just a fraction out. Really good girls unpick, some swear under their breath (usually oaths such as 'Sugar!' or 'Flip!'; we quilters are really a very genteel lot ...). We bodgers, though, try and think of a way of disguising the bad join – and buttons are just perfect.

Most of us have fond memories of riffling through our mother's button tin; it was lovely just sorting them into different colours, shapes and sizes, or threading them on a string to make a necklace. I rarely actually buy buttons: I tend to cut them from old clothes – men's shirts are great for this, and nowadays when you buy a garment they nearly always give you a spare button. It's much more fun to use these on quilts than actually keep them for their proper purpose; as I've said, isn't that what safety pins are for?! If you want to buy, though, there are specialist suppliers selling buttons in all sorts of shapes and patterns which can add real interest to your quilts.

Last year I came to the conclusion that I really was getting too mean, going to jumble sales to buy old shirts for the sake of the buttons, and decided to buy in bulk. I contacted a button manufacturer in Leicester; they sold me a box of assorted pearl buttons for a very modest price, and I think they might last my lifetime. I was rather amazed a few months later when a man appeared at my door with a rep's suitcase; I thought he was bringing sample bricks or some other thrilling item for our surveying business. He said that he was the button representative for the whole of the south of England and had travelled up from Bourne- mouth (150 miles); he obviously thought that I made garments. I was so embarrassed that I did offer him coffee before telling him of my lifetime's supply.

Top left: a perfect use for assorted beads!

Bottom left: button eyes on a detail of They Must be Useful for Something

Above: detail of Zoë's Quilt

Below: any child can have fun making a button quilt like this one – see page 19

I used pearl buttons on *Fragments from the Sun* to cover up some nasty joins. I made the quilt using cyanotype printing (described on page 35; I'm sure you'll want to try it if you aren't familiar with the technique); it was the first time I'd tried it, and I was using every scrap of fabric I had prepared. I printed everything I could lay my hands on, including leaves, feathers, scissors and even the net washing bags which come with every box of washing tablets. I then ended up with a heap of fabric of disparate sizes and couldn't decide which ones to use in the quilt.

In the end I chose all the leaves, flowers, feathers and lace and just sewed the pieces together randomly, to give the effect of Delft tiles. This resulted in some rather unfortunate mis-joins. Remembering my pearl button collection, I stitched one over each bad join, then I realised that I had to add more buttons to make the effect look more 'designed' and intentional. The buttons give a sparkle and added interest to the quilt, and turned the mistake into a design opportunity.

If you're facing the same problem, lay the quilt on the floor and place buttons on the joins where you think they ought to go; then stand back, have a good look, and possibly take a tea break. Then when you return and see it afresh, the balance of the buttons and where they should go becomes clearer. Pin them in position, or make a mark with a soft pencil or soap; otherwise, when you pick up the quilt and they all fall off you won't remember where you intended them to go.

Zoë's quilt

I introduced you to Zoë in *Quirky Quilts;* she nobly posed with a knife and fork. I made her a very rushed wall quilt when she was born, created out of a chopped-up printed alphabet panel (yes, I'm not proud; I use anything in my quilts!) I know I should have drafted out the alphabet myself and spent ages appliquéing it to the quilt, but I was more interested in being a 'hands-on' Grandma and she might have been 18 before I finished a more labour-intensive quilt.

The blocks in between are pictures to correspond with the

letters; these I bonded and oversewed. I used the printed panel alphabet squares as a guide to the size of each block, but when I came to assemble them found they didn't quite fit. So, once again a button on each join created a sparkle effect and covered the evidence. The queen with the handbag is quite a favourite with the girls!

Sewing buttons in decorative ways

You can stitch the buttons on in many different ways to add extra interest to your quilt: try some of these ideas (shown in the illustrations).

- Attach each button with brightly-coloured stranded cotton. Buttons with four holes can be sewn either with two straight stitches, in a cross shape, or in a square design.

- Stitch a smaller button on top of a large one to add depth.

- Use thin ribbon instead of thread and then tie it in a bow for a decoration.

- Radiate the stitches outwards from the button for a different effect.

I used buttons in my quilt *Irrational Prejudices* as sashing joins. As the main motif was a cross I made crosses of pearl buttons between the blocks to accentuate the theme.

Buttons in lieu of quilting

I make lots of crazy quilts and sometimes it's difficult to know how to quilt them; often there's so much embroidery stitching and surface decoration that hand quilting would be impossible and machine stitching inappropriate. So buttons are a really useful way of holding the three layers together. In my quilt *It's Not all Hearts and Flowers* I used this technique and chose buttons appropriate to each panel.

Beads for bodges

Beads can also be used as above and can add a sparkle to a quilt. As with buttons, beads are better used on wall hangings rather than bed quilts, as it might be a bit nasty sitting on a protruding button or bead in your flimsy night attire!

Beads can't disguise a bad join in the way a button can, but can be very useful to accentuate the place where one block joins to another. For example, in my log cabin quilt *Ghosts* I used bleached black fabric for the light strips and the plain black fabric for the dark strips. (I showed you how to make the easy bleached effects in *Quirky Quilts* page 59.) Some of the 'light' squares came out rather dark, so, as the centre squares were red, I added small red beads at the corners to accentuate the blocks.

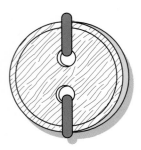

Child's button quilt

Zoë made her own first quilt with buttons when she was five; it's shown on page 17. The method she used is an idea you might like to try with small children. This is a relatively naive quilt as I feel strongly that small children should be allowed to make handicraft things themselves. I used to be saddened when my children came out of

playgroup with beautifully crafted objects which I knew the teacher had made for them.

One of our treasured possessions is a Christmas tree angel made by one of the boys from a toilet-roll middle; she has a wonky smile and a badly-fitting doily dress, and still gets pride of place at the top of the tree.

1

4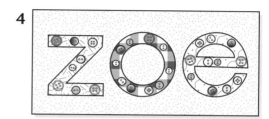

2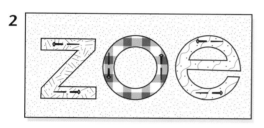

5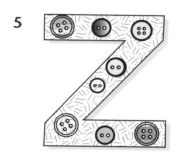

3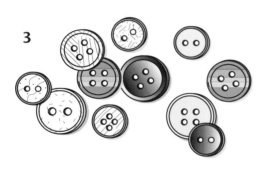

6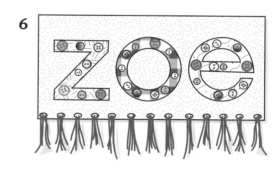

1 Cut out each letter of the name from fabric (preferably a fabric that's not too openweave to avoid fraying). You could use felt. It was easy for me with a three-letter name, so if her name is Charlotte-Louise you have a bigger job on your hands!

2 Pin or tack the letters to a brightly-coloured backing fabric or a piece of furnishing fabric (we used some velvet curtaining).

3 Let the child loose on your button tin, or buy packets from charity shops. The child will choose the buttons he or she

likes best; varied shapes, colours, textures and sizes add to the fun.

4 Thread up a large needle with double thread knotted at the end (if you don't have it double they will keep on pulling too hard and you will spend your entire time re-threading the needle). Teach the child how to sew on the button on top of the name.

5 Stitch four or five buttons on each letter to hold it down. The child soon gets the hang of putting the needle up in the right place and then down into the back. It's also a useful skill to

learn, as they might grow up to be more conscientious than Grandma and want to sew lost buttons back onto their clothes!

6 The final touch was to make a fringe along the bottom out of bits of ribbon. If you keep ribbons from Christmas gifts, bouquets of flowers or boxes of chocolates they'll always come in useful for something. (Florists sell very cheap ribbon, which they use to make up bows on bouquets; it's made so that you can rip it into any width, and at a few pence a metre would be ideal for this job.)

It's astonishing how many different ways there are to cut, combine and add colour and pattern to fabric. Over the years I've learned some fascinating techniques, along with all kinds of clever tricks which make quilting both easier and more fun!

Wherever I go, quilters are intrigued by novel techniques such as the blue printing (see below) and the leaf hammering (which I talked about in *Quirky Quilts)* I was once trying to explain leaf hammering to a party of French women at a quilt show. One lady was the translator for the rest of them, which was fine until we got to 'soak in washing soda;' she looked very blank, so I tried explaining that it can be used for unblocking sinks. Having just scraped through GCE French in the dark ages, I realised that I didn't know the words either for 'blocked' or for 'sink.' So I hit on a really good idea: I would draw a blocked sink. Unfortunately my drawing looked a bit like a bent wine glass; 'Oh, yes: whisky and soda' the lady said, translating to the eagerly awaiting friends. Luckily someone then came up with *cristaux de saude.*

It's actually great fun being an 'expert' at shows; there's a sort of camaraderie with the other 'experts,' and I've made some lovely friends who previously were only quilting names to me. There's the funny side to all this exposure as well, of course; some people speak about you and your work as if you weren't there, even though you're wearing a name label. It always brings me down to earth when I hear something like 'Oh, it's that Dorothy Stapleton: she does those funny quilts, but I don't like them.' There are lots of nice comments too, though, and it's always good to have feedback on your work – I'm always pleased when I can introduce people to clever techniques they've never tried before.

It's great chatting to other quilters, too, at shows and at talks, and finding out what they're involved in. So when you come across we 'experts' at shows, please do come and talk us. As demonstrators we're often at a bit of a disadvantage, though; as I go all over the place giving talks, people remember my name as I was the clown standing on the stage at the front, but it's quite tricky for me to remember all those nice ladies in the audience. So remember too that it'll make our conversations much more interesting (and meaningful) if you remind me where we've met before! And don't be intimidated; you are the one doing the careful immaculate work, while I'm the one covering over my mistakes with a smile ...

This section of the book shows you some of the tricks and dodges I've learned over the years. They're so useful, I don't want to keep them all to myself, so dip in and share them!

Below: detail of Algarve Spring, *log cabin stitched over a grid*

Opposite top: my quilt What Shall We Call It? *made use of quick appliqué, machine writing and the envelope method!*

Opposite below: blue printing

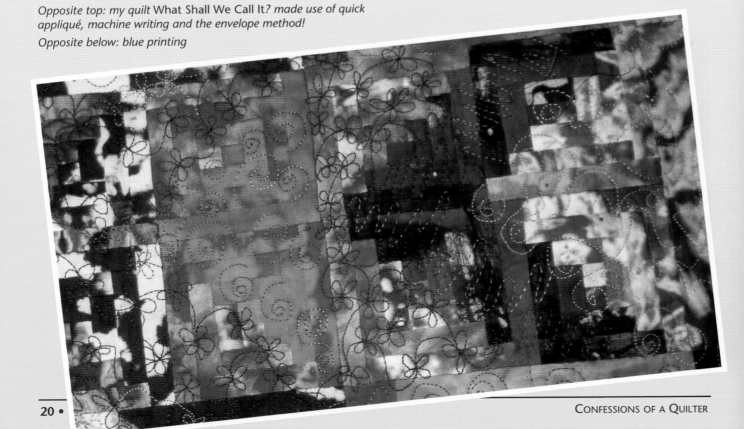

Writing with the machine

is a personal quirk of mine. I'm not suggesting that you write stuff all over your quilts if that's not your style, but it's a useful skill for anyone because you can create your own labels, and it's great for personalising children's quilts.

Easy appliqué

demonstrates two quick and easy ways of doing accurate appliqué. The first method uses freezer paper; it's very accurate, and the same pattern can be re-used for quite a time, so it saves effort too. And for a real short cut, try the second method: bonding web appliqué.

Accurate log cabin the easy way

explains how you can get that enviable accuracy by using a grid foundation. This method is done by hand, so you can take it round with you to fill up those odd moments.

Blue printing

is great fun, and creates superb effects. It may seem daunting when you hear that it requires scary-sounding chemicals, but just follow the instructions and you'll be amazed at the fantastic patterns you will make with only the sun to help you.

The envelope method

is my personal hobby-horse, as I think it makes the joining of a large quilt or hanging so much easier. Anyone making a group quilt will find this section invaluable, as the method means that each block is *quilted* as well as pieced!

Writing with the machine

I love adding writing to my quilts, partly to add silly quips to make myself and other quilters laugh, and also I find it a nice way of quilting backgrounds. My first attempt was in *I'm Only a Mum* (see page 3); I wrote Mummy, Mother, Ma, Mum in a continuous line, using a black thread on a green background. This created the effect of a continuous quilting pattern. Since then I've added machine-quilted writing to several other quilts; some people think it looks tricky, but it's actually very easy once you get into the rhythm.

In *What Shall We Call It?* (see page 27) I used yellow thread on a green background. In *Baby Talk* the quilting was more subtle; I quilted Babytalk in yellow thread on a yellow background. (Maybe too subtle, as the hours of hard work hardly showed up, but I know the words are there!) I feel that a nice touch in a quilt is not to see all the intricacies in one go. It's good to have the first visual impact; then as you get closer you find the little, nearly hidden, subtle touches.

I write freehand, so if I'm using a long word I have to make sure that it will fit in the allotted space. This, of course, doesn't always work, and it's very difficult to unpick machine quilting. You'll notice, on my quilts that feature writing, that there are some little doodles of flowers in amongst the words; this is where the word was too short to fill the allotted space! (Making a feature out of the mistake yet again.) If you don't feel brave enough to write freehand, try marking where the word begins with hard soap or crayon – I suppose you could draw the words out and quilt over the marked line, but to me the essence of machine quilting is a nice, loose, free movement and flowing lines.

There is no magic formula to machine writing (unless you have a programmable machine that does it for you!) Doing it freehand recreates that individuality that we all have in our personal handwriting. Basically, it's practice makes perfect; the more you do it the better you become, until it's second nature. The easiest way to describe what's happening is to think of the machine needle as your pencil and the fabric as your paper – but instead of moving the pencil over the paper, the pencil is static and the paper is moving.

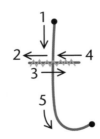

crossing the t

method a:
stitch down to the cross, then stitch from side to side and back to the centre; finally, finish the stem

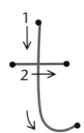

method b:
stitch from the top to the bottom of the stem, then come back and cross the t in a separate line

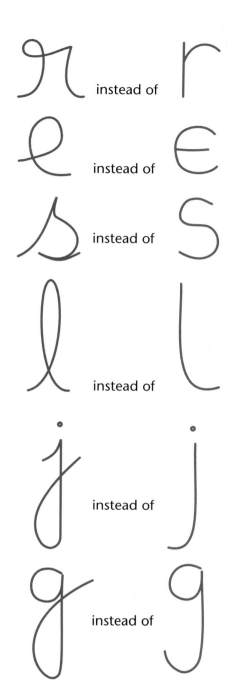

instead of r

instead of e

instead of s

instead of l

instead of j

instead of g

dotted i's and j's are hand-sewn French knots

yes you can do it ~ just practise

Method

Sit comfortably at your machine; an office chair is ideal for this as you can adjust the height and back rest, and swivel round to iron your patches. (These chairs are regularly advertised very cheaply in small ads in the local paper, and out of date models are often sold off by office supply shops.) Another very simple tip is: sit directly opposite the machine. This sounds like common sense, but if you check, quite often you'll find that your chair is slightly to one side of the machine; this means that you're constantly twisting your back just a fraction, which can cause aches and pains.

You don't need a fancy machine with all the whiz-bangs to do machine writing; all you need is a darning foot. You actually don't even need this, but it safeguards you from sewing through your finger: ouch! Even we 'experts' do this; I was lucky – the needle went in and out and it was just a painful experience, but I have heard of stitchers having to go to the hospital to have a needle removed. A precaution might be to have sticking plasters next to the machine ...

The feed dogs – the little teeth which pull the fabric along – need to be down on the machine. (If your machine doesn't have this facility the manufacturers usually provide a plate to fit over the feed dogs.) If you don't know how to lower the feed dogs, look in your machine manual; that's that useful book which you read through once when you bought the machine! Lowering them means that the machine isn't pulling the fabric along; you are controlling the length of the stitch and its direction by the speed and angle at which you're guiding the fabric under the foot.

When you start, bring the bobbin thread up to the top so you can see where it is; otherwise you might be writing all over it and getting in a nasty tangle underneath. Use the same-coloured thread on the top and in the bobbin for an easier life; this means that if your tension is slightly out it won't show. If your machine will go half-speed, turn on this facility. The general object is to press the foot down hard, so that the machine is at full speed, and then turn the fabric as slowly as possible to get small, neat stitches. Therefore by halving the speed you have more control. Practise gliding the fabric around, not stopping and starting; I promise you, it gets easier with practice. Relax your wrists, and move the fabric around smoothly with your fingertips. Some quilters use special gloves for this; they look like gardening gloves but have rubber tips to cling onto the fabric, and they apparently stop repetitive strain injuries.

You're aiming for a continuous line of stitches, so the best kind of writing to use is the old-fashioned loopy type (top left). Get out your old autograph book, and I bet if it's like mine you'll have some wonderful loopy entries. When I was at school we were initially taught to write using flourishes and loops, but then had that drummed out of us and had to write in the Marion Richardson style (presumably she was an educationalist). This was with no loops or curly bits, and non-continuous;

nowadays children are taught to write like this from the start. You can machine-write like this and not use loops, but you'll have to go back and forwards more times. (See the diagrams.)

It's well worth the perseverance to learn how to write with your machine; even if you don't want to write things on your quilts – and most people aren't as zany as me – you could make labels for your quilts. Signing them by machine is a lot quicker than painstakingly embroidering your name by hand, especially when you have a long name like mine.

Above: in this detail of What Shall We Call It? *you can see some of the flower-name suggestions behind the mother*

Below: the close-up of Baby Talk *shows the all-over background writing in yellow, and the contrast writing that I stitched above each baby's face and below each carrycot*

I demonstrate at quilt shows, and sometimes they hang a quilt beside the table rather than behind it. I was sitting just round the corner from *What Shall We Call It?*, which has a complete background of written names (see page 27, and detail above). As people came through the door they couldn't see me tucked in round the corner; it was quite interesting hearing the comments. Usually hair-raising birth experiences! But I was moved to jump up and protest when I heard: 'She has a programmable machine, you know; she doesn't do any of that writing herself.' I had to tell them that 'yes I jolly well do, and it takes ages!'

Quick appliqué

Most quilters love the look of appliqué, whether it's done by hand or machine, but I've met many people who feel that they aren't skilled (or neat!) enough to do appliqué quilts themselves. If you're one of those people, this section has got your name on it ...

There are two main ways of doing appliqué which make it astonishingly quick and simple; I use them both in my quilts. The first involves that magical stuff called freezer paper; you may have wondered why a catering product is sold in quilt shops and at the shows, and this technique is the answer. There are various different methods of freezer paper appliqué (for full coverage, have a peep at Dawn Cameron-Dick's book *Invisible Machine Appliqué*, also published by Teamwork Craftbooks), but here I'll explain the most straightforward one that I was taught to do a few years ago.

Freezer paper appliqué

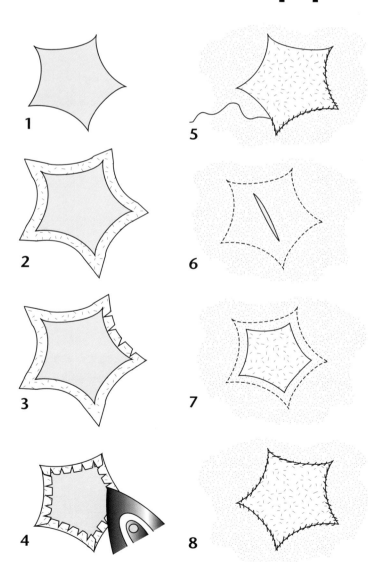

1   Cut each shape that you want to appliqué from freezer paper. The paper has two sides, shiny and dull; for this technique, cut each shape with the dull side right side up.

2   Pin each freezer paper shape to the appropriate fabric, dull side of the paper to the wrong side of the fabric, and cut the fabric to shape leaving a ¼in allowance all round.

3   Clip any inside curves; you don't need to clip outside curves.

4   With the tip of a warm iron, press the seam allowances over the edges of the paper shape; the fabric will stick temporarily to the shiny side of the freezer paper.

5   You now have an appliqué piece which you can stitch to your background fabric, using either hand or machine stitching.

6   When the appliqué is complete, make a small slit on the back of the work inside the stitched shape.

7   Remove the piece of freezer paper through the slit. (if you're using the same shape again in your design, you may be able to re-use the freezer paper template.) If you wish, trim the background fabric ¼in inside the stitched line.

8   The finished appliquéd patch.

A couple of years ago I was asked to make a quilt for the Knitting and Stitching Show's Quilt 99 exhibition. They wrote and said that the subject would be Great Expectations; I immediately thought of a row of pregnant women holding their aching backs. I made a repetitive pattern with freezer paper for the faces, bodies and wombs, and made the quilt in separate units using the envelope method (see page 40).

I then thought of the ideal theme: the unexpected outcome of pre-naming a baby. My three boys were all to be called Sophie, as this was in the days before scans and knowing the sex of the baby before birth. The outer quilted names are the proposed names, and the actual name is on the baby.

There are eight mothers; from left to right they are as follows.

THE HIPPY with proposed names:
India, Leaf, Wave, Saffron, Ziggy, Swampy, Eclipse (I was sewing this panel on the day of the solar eclipse), Surf, Trixybelle, Little Flower, Cloud, Tempest, Star, Moonflower, Sky, Willow, Indigo, Saffron. The actual baby is Bob.

TWINS: these are twosomes, or names that are in some way associated with each other.
Oscar & Lucinda, Bill & Ben (*The Flowerpot Men* – children's TV characters), Janet & John (the early reading scheme); Eric & Ernie (the comedians Morecombe and Wise), Ronnie & Reggie (the gangster Kray twins), Romulus & Remus, Barbie & Ken (the dolls), Bonnie & Clyde, Shula & Kenton (twins in *The Archers*, a long-running radio soap opera), Victoria & Albert, Pinky & Perky (cartoon pigs). The actual twins are called Pip and Estella – the characters in the book *Great Expectations*.

JEWEL NAMES:
Ruby, Jet, Jade, Amber, Pearl, Silver, Precious, Diamond, Amethyst, Coral, Goldie, Sparkle, Jewel, Topaz, Sapphire, Emerald. The actual baby is Rock. While I was demonstrating at the Knitting and Stitching show in London a lady and her little boy came up to speak to me. He said 'Excuse me, I'm on your quilt; my name's Rock!' He was so thrilled; he thought I'd done it just for him.

SHAKESPEARIAN NAMES:
Claudius, Alice, Juno, Lysander, Titania, Juliet, Horatio, Hermia, Harry, Portia, Edmund, Ophelia, Marcus, Rosalind, Puck, Brutus, Hamlet, Cassius, Katherine, Orlando, Malcolm, Celia, Lewis. The actual boy is Gary.

QUADS: these are foursomes.
Matthew, Mark, Luke & John. Paul, John, George & Ringo. TinkyWinky, Dipsy, LaLa & Po (*The Teletubbies* children's TV characters) – I actually had to ring a friend and ask for the fourth Teletubby's name! Then as I was sewing it I read in the paper that there was to be a new programme called *The Tweenies*, and their names are also included: Bella, Milo, Fizz & Jake. Groucho, Harpo, Zeppo & Chico (the Marx Brothers). The actual quads are Louis, Tina, Nina & Ella (black singers).

BIBLICAL NAMES:
Job, Abraham, Isaac, Jonathan, Timothy, Joshua, Moses, Thomas, Jacob, Jabez, David, James, Bartholomew, Solomon, Joseph, Lazarus, Noah, Barnabas, Cornelius. (When Zoë had been at school a little while we were discussing names, and I suggested she was lucky that her name was easy to write with three letters. She said 'We can all spell our names except Cornelius.') The actual baby is called Fifi.

TRIPLETS: these were a total nightmare – when I had racked my brains for threesomes I realised that Tom, Dick and Harry would have done. The threesomes are:

Flopsy, Mopsy & Cottontail (Peter Rabbit's siblings); Faith, Hope & Charity; Freeman, Hardy & Willis (a well-known chain of shoe shops); Tiny, Tilly & Tom (children's TV characters); Mary, Mungo & Midge (also TV characters of the time when my children were small); Snap, Crackle and Pop (the Rice Krispies cereal characters). The actual names are Trio, Trios and Tres, all meaning three in various languages.

FLOWER NAMES:

Jonquil, Azalea, Hyacinth, Marigold, Poppy, Lily, Rose, Heather, Angelica, Daisy, Violet, Primrose, Rosemary, Flora, Holly, Rosie. The baby is called Tom.

It was actually these flower names that first got me thinking: I have some great nieces called Flora, Poppy and Posie, and they have a friend called Peony. I'll now own up to my three sons' names in case you were wondering. They're all on the quilt; no not Romulus, Puck and Jabez – they are Paul, Matthew and Tom. I realised after trying to write Matthew Stapleton in a two-year-old's Wellington boot the value of a short name, so the next and last one is Tom.

The border is made from crazy-pieced children's fabrics, left over from various floor-quilt projects for grandchildren and great-nieces and -nephews. I machined between and over the patches with a sort of buttonhole fancy stitch on my machine. I herringbone-stitched by hand between the blocks in yellow stranded thread as the quilt was looking a bit dark, and added a smaller herringbone stitch between the edge of the blocks and the border.

This is a quilt people either love or hate; some people think it a rather distasteful theme for a quilt and others just love it. It won the first prize and trophy for humour at Quilts UK 2000. Many quilters are nurses or midwives, and many people expressed a wish to have the quilt in their hospital scanning room or pre-natal clinic. So I had cards and posters printed and have sold them in aid of Bliss, the baby life support charity. It has already raised over £500 for them and is continuing to do so. So it might not be to everyone's taste but it has done some good.

The second quick-and-easy appliqué method involves double-sided bonding web, sold under several brand names including Bondaweb and Heat 'n' Bond. This method tends to work best with machine appliqué; you can stitch the pieces on by hand, but because the raw edges aren't actually turned under, the stitching may pull through the fabric, or the edges of the shape may fray more than you want.

Bonding web appliqué

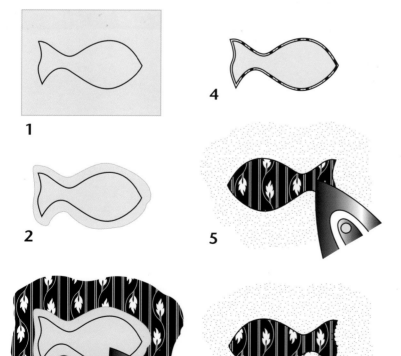

1 Trace each shape you want to appliqué onto the paper side of the bonding web; because of the way this method works, you'll need to reverse any asymmetric shapes.

2 Cut roughly round the outside of each individual shape, leaving a small allowance. (If you're going to bond several shapes to the same fabric, you can leave them in one piece.)

3 Lay the bonding web shape, rough side down, onto the wrong side of the appropriate fabric; fuse the pieces into place with a warm iron.

4 Cut round each shape along the marked line.

5 Peel off the backing paper and lay the appliqué piece, web side down, onto the background fabric. Fuse into place with a warm iron.

6 Stitch round the edges by hand or by machine.

Accurate log cabin the easy way!

I've had a long-standing love affair with log cabin patchwork: I think it's my thrifty (or mean) trait of trying to use every scrap of available fabric. Also, you don't need templates – and there are so many designs that can be achieved from just stitching strips round a central square.

I realised a few years ago that I think I have a sort of spatial dyslexia. In a psychology class when they showed the classic shape of two faces or a vase, I was the only person who really couldn't see the two faces. When I try and put traditional patchwork blocks together I can't seem to realise which bit goes where. I then thought, why bother? I don't have to make quilts in traditional blocks. So now I usually only make quilts with log cabin blocks, or silly quilts with appliqué. Another disaster turned into an opportunity; people now call it my 'style.'

As I went on creating log cabin quilts I found that they were getting smaller and considerably less accurate. I had cut up bagfuls of 1in strips for my log cabin houses (see *Quirky Quilts,* page 36) in various colours and patterns, and was using those to create blocks. Inaccuracy is a major hazard of log cabin for us bodgers; as each block progresses a minor inaccuracy becomes worse and worse as more rows are added. My sewing machine seems suddenly to get a mind of its own when I get to the end of a seam and veers off to the left. (Or could it be its operator, who thinks 'Good! I'm at the end of a seam' and takes her eye off the ball, as it were?) Then I discovered gridded Vilene: by using the grid on a checked fabric as a sewing guide, log cabin suddenly becomes as easy as falling off a log.

The only snag with this gridded Vilene is that it only comes in a centimetre grid; therefore, if you want larger 'logs' you have to go over two or three squares at a time. This isn't much of a drawback, though, and is extremely useful for curved log cabin designs (see *Quirky Quilts* page 44).

If you want to make a cheaty miniature log cabin quilt, men's shirts make an ideal grid for the foundation. With any checked fabric that you're buying or using, though, do make sure that the grid is truly accurate: gingham can look perfectly square but may be woven a fraction out of true, and this causes difficulties when you're sewing the blocks together. Men's shirts are easily available either from your family or from charity shops (you can use the buttons for the bodgy corners of blocks – see page 16).

Do make sure that your husband knows you have chopped up his shirt. I was told by a quilter that her husband retired from the city so, unbeknown to him, she used his white shirts for various dyeing projects. When he was going to a funeral he searched for a white shirt to wear and wasn't best pleased to hear of their fate. Somehow a Hawaiian short-sleeved job didn't have the same sober effect.

My quilt *Obsession* (see page 33) uses the grid and it means that the strength of the fabric is all in the backing, so fabrics that are usually considered unsuitable for patchwork, such as lawn, lamé, silk, wool and stretchy fabrics, can be used.

The other beauty of this method of log cabin is that it can be sewn by

Log cabin on gridded fabric

These instructions will make a square 9x9cm. Use 1in (2.5cm) wide fabric strips throughout.

1 Cut a piece of gridded Vilene 9 squares by 9 squares.

2 Cut a 2cm square of fabric and position it right side up on the wrong side of the Vilene grid. Cover the central square so that there's an even border all round; pin it in place. This will become the middle of your log cabin block.

3 Cut a strip of 'light' fabric to length and pin it along one edge of the central fabric square so that the raw edges align, right sides together. Stitch a seam, by hand or machine, along the grid line. (You can stitch from the other side if you find it easier.)

4 Fold the fabric strip back so that the right side shows and press the seam.

5 Pin and stitch another 'light' strip along the next side in the same way.

6 Fold this strip back and press it as before.

7 Add a 'dark' strip to the third side in the same way.

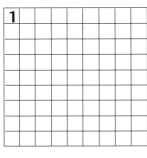

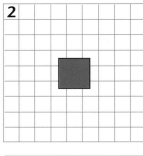

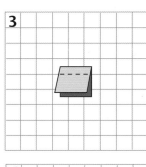

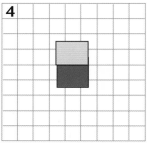

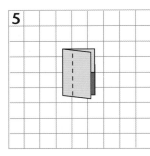

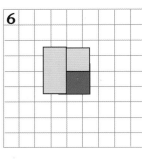

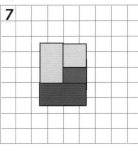

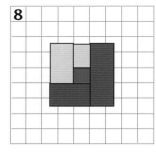

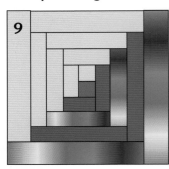

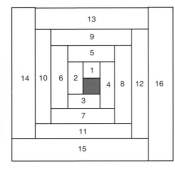

8 Complete the first circuit with a 'dark' strip on the fourth side.

9 Continue adding strips round the sides of the square, following the order on the numbered diagram, making four complete circuits in total. Remember to add 'light' strips to two sides and 'dark' strips to the other two. When you've finished adding the strips, you'll have a 5mm seam allowance overlapping each edge of the Vilene square.

hand. Shock horror! I know you'll be saying, 'she's perfectly mad! How would you have time for this kind of project?' Time is the whole advantage of this method, though; it can be done in those spare useless moments: waiting in the car, at stations, in doctors' and hospital waiting rooms, while watching TV, and generally when you can't think of anything creative to do. In fact it's 'on-the-go' sewing.

I made my double bed quilt *Just In Case of Hijack* (opposite) by hand over a period of ten years in spare moments. The fashion now is to make quilts in a day or a weekend, but I think it's always good to have a 'life's work' on the go. The only stipulation is to live long enough to finish it, but even that needn't be a problem; imagine some relative sorting out your quilting after your demise and thinking 'this looks good: I'll finish it off!' – so passing on the skills to the next generation.

Above: Just In Case of Hijack

Just in Case of Hijack was so named after my friend from New Zealand was staying and, as she was leaving for the airport said 'I'll just put my hijack knickers in my handbag.' I thought it was a good idea, so now I take my spare knickers and some sewing. Imagine what a blow if you were hijacked for days, thinking of all that sewing you could have been doing. This quilt – or pieces of it – visited many paces during those ten years; it went to Australia twice to visit my son in Perth, to the USA on holiday, and accompanied me on many hospital visits to my very elderly blind father. It was real sanity sewing; he kept on apologising for taking up so much of my precious time, but it didn't matter – I was getting on with my sewing and not feeling resentful. Also, it's a more enjoyable occupation in the waiting room than four-year-old copies of *Hello magazine*. I think I should explain that I only took the individual 9x9cm squares with me, as it wasn't a double bed quilt at this stage. That's the big advantage of this method: it's very portable.

I didn't even know when I was making it that it was going to be stars. I just made bags and bags of squares in blues and browns as those are the colours I love; I think it's because I taught batik wax resist class for 15 years, and the old Javanese batiks tend to be blues and browns. When I had a few carrier bags full of squares I put them on the bed and jiggled them around, and realised I could make an Ohio star shape; I then had large spare squares between them which could make another star block. I then did a frightening sum and realised how many more blocks needed to be made: the final total is 640. I actually drew it out on squared paper, which is rather more organised than usual.

Right: this is how I created the pattern of different-sized stars in Just In Case of Hijack; *just continue joining blocks in this basic design to create the required number of small and large stars.*

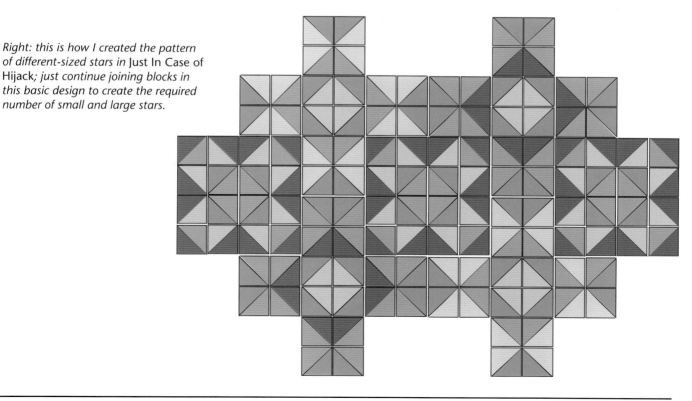

Frightening sums have gone down in our family folklore. My middle son came home in tears from primary school, aged 5. I eventually got out of him what had happened; he said 'there was a frightening sum on the blackboard.' I had a word with the teacher, who laughed and said that it was a multiplication sum for some older children, which had nothing to do with him at all. I know his problem, though; I've always found sums frightening, and I still count on my fingers (this can cause embarrassment in the bank). Thank God for calculators.

How to make a log cabin keyring

If you don't think you can spare the odd ten years for a bedspread, the star pattern on page 31 could be made into a cushion. Or you can really chicken out and just make a keyring out of one block! Actually these make really nice little presents for quilting friends or for fund-raising events. Any men in the house won't want to borrow your keys if they're on a patchwork keyring.

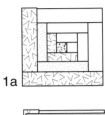 1a

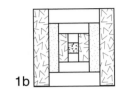 1b

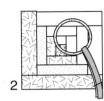 2

 3

 4

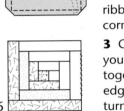 5   6

1 Begin with one log cabin (a) or courthouse steps (b) block made over gridded Vilene.

2 Put a keyring on a loop of narrow ribbon and stitch the loop to one corner of the block to secure it.

3 Cut a square of backing fabric to fit your block, lay the squares right sides together, and stitch a seam round the edges, leaving a small opening for turning.

4 Clip the corners.

5 Turn to the right side.

6 Slipstitch the opening closed.

Using the grid for multi-sized blocks

The other boon about the gridded fabric is that you can vary the sizes of the strips and blocks and they'll still magically fit together, which is a great boon for mathematical dunces like me. I used this effect in my quilt *Ghosts,* which was made from all the leftover bits of bleached black fabric from a log cabin comforter.

I also used different-sized blocks in *Algarve Spring* (opposite right); this also used up all the leftover samples of various coloured fabrics I'd tried bleaching. We regularly visit the Algarve in Portugal in springtime; the flowers are fantastic, and as you walk on the cliffs there are fields of wild iris and lupins. I wanted to convey the feeling and colours of the flowers in the log cabin blocks; I free-machined quilted flowers over the strips in rainbow variegated cottons.

I seem to have trouble with leftovers of every kind; I can't seem to throw anything away. I'm the same with food; I'm always trying to concoct a meal out of the day before's remains. I shudder if I'm visiting my family, when my son will throw the remains of the roast chicken in the kitchen bin; I've even been known to take it home for soup (saved before it got to the bin; I'm not that bad!). I'm afraid I do retrieve fabric from bins, though; you'd be amazed at what students throw away during a class. One person's rubbish is another person's treasure.

Above left: Obsession, *made from Liberty lawn scraps over men's shirting*
Left: log cabin keyring, made from one block Above right: Algarve Spring

Our town rubbish tip used to have a system that allowed you to take anything home which had been dumped there. When the boys were young we tipped our hedge clippings there one day and saw a go-kart sitting on the rubbish heap. The boys were thrilled: we took it home, and they drove up and down the pavement feeling very proud. We were slightly embarrassed, though, when a neighbour two doors up said 'I've just taken that to the dump; I would have given it to you if I'd known you wanted it ...'

These are the basic log cabin units I used to create Obsession *(above left); you can see that the centres of a and e cover four squares of the grid rather than one. I did the large centre block (e) as a courthouse steps block to balance the overall design. The chart on page 34 shows how the different-sized units build up into the complete quilt.*

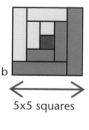

b

5x5 squares

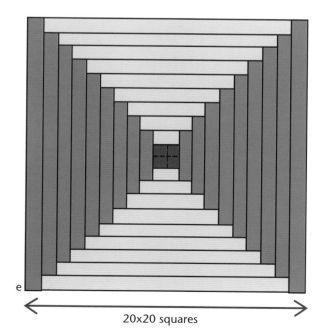

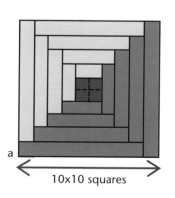

c

d

a

10x10 squares

e

20x20 squares

The layout for Obsession *(shown on page 33, with the basic blocks used to create it), showing how the different-sized blocks are combined to create the whole quilt*

When you're using the grid over two squares it's easier to machine the blocks, as the strips are now 2in (5cm) wide and so not as fiddly as the 1in-wide ones. You still have the option of hand-sewing, though. I made *Algarve Spring* by both hand and machine, depending on which was most convenient at the time.

I achieved the different-sized blocks in *Obsession* (see page 33) quite by accident. Sometimes a happy accident can really make the quilt more interesting, and this was a case in point. In some blocks the central red square is over four of the grid squares, but in the smaller blocks the central square only covers one grid square; therefore, four small blocks ended up being the same size as one large one. Not a bad mistake for an innumerate dumdum like me ...

Blue printing

Now it's time for The Science Bit!

The real name for this technique of printing with the sun is *cyanotype*. It originated in the 1840s as a method of photographic reproduction, and was developed (!) by Sir John Herschel only three years after photography as we now know it had been invented. It was originally known as Prussian blue printing, as Herschel was German.

The principle is that the fabric is treated with chemicals so that it then becomes light-sensitive like photographic paper. When the fabric is then put in bright sunlight it 'develops' and turns bright blue. You create patterns on the blue background by placing objects – or a photographic negative – on the fabric while it's in the sun; as the blue colour develops on the exposed fabric, it leaves a white imprint where the sun has been blocked. The developing process takes from 5 to 15 minutes, depending on the intensity of the sun; you then leave the fabric in running water to flush out the chemicals, and an image appears as if by magic!

I first saw this technique three or four years ago when I was host for an American quilter, Carol Adleman, who was visiting our quilt group from Minnesota. She gave me some printed fabric and the recipe for soaking the fabric. When the summer came I eagerly rang some chemical suppliers from Yellow Pages and was alarmed to be told that the things I wanted were dangerous chemicals and not available to the individual, only to laboratories. Luckily, two years ago at the National Patchwork Championships I met a quilter who was using blue printing in her work, and she told me how to obtain the chemicals by post.

Amazingly the weather turned up trumps, which is a rare thing in England in July, and we had a heat wave; I had such fun messing with my blue prints. There is a delightful urgency about it, as you never know when the sun is going to disappear for days. I also bought a scientific book on the process (see page 72), and was pleased to read that the chemicals were quite harmless if used and stored properly. Take sensible precautions, protecting work surfaces and your skin; work in well-ventilated areas, avoid inhaling fumes, and follow all the manufacturers' safety instructions for the different chemicals.

Recipe for preparing the fabric

- *Ferric ammonium citrate (yellow-green)*

- *Potassium ferricyanide (orange-red crystals) That's the one that sounds very scary ...*

- *Distilled water, obtainable from garages or cycle shops (it's used for topping up car batteries)*

- *Two brown or green bottles for keep the stock solution (I used sherry bottles!). They need to be dark to keep the light out*

- *A measuring jug (not one you use for cooking! Always keep the utensils you use for blue printing separate)*

- *An old bowl or large dish*

- *A strong plastic bag to use with your kitchen scales – or keep an old set of scales solely for dyeing and other chemical processes*

- *Washed calico or sheeting, 100% cotton*

Making the stock solutions

Make up two separate bottles of stock solution:

Stock 1

2oz (60g) of ferric ammonium citrate (yellow-green) in 8fl oz (250ml) of distilled water. Make this in a small bowl; mix it with a plastic spoon and pour into one of the brown or green bottles.

Stock 2

1oz (30g) of potassium ferricyanide in 8fl oz (250ml) of distilled water; mix and store as above.

Mark each bottle clearly with a sticky label and write on the contents and the date. The stock solutions will keep for about six months; the dry chemicals will keep indefinitely, but remember to store them safely out of the reach of children and away from your food storage areas.

Preparing the fabric

When you are ready to prepare the fabric, mix equal amounts of the two solutions in a plastic bowl or dish; this will stain it, so make sure it's only used for this purpose.

I find that cutting my fabric into A4-sized pieces, or smaller, makes the process easier to handle. The fabric has to be soaked and dried in a very low light or it will 'develop,' just as photographic paper does. I initially thought that it should be completely dark and, as I couldn't wait for nightfall to get on with it, I used my internal shower room which has no window. This was somewhat hilarious, trying to rig up a makeshift washing line between the shower and the toilet, propping the door open a whisker with one foot so that I could just about see and not suffocate, as it's a very small room; inelegantly kneeling with my bottom in the air, dripping blue gunge all over the floor.

Having put myself through all this trauma I re-read Carol's instructions

Top left: Fragments of the Sun

Bottom left: detail of Sewing in the Sun

This page, top: A Tapestry of Birds

This page, above: cardboard shapes, twigs and leaves ready for blue printing, plus some finished samples

and found that it said a 60-watt bulb and no direct sunlight. So for future batches I used a blinds-down room with a low-watt table lamp.

Wear rubber gloves and soak each piece of fabric in the solution in the bowl. Squeeze out the fabric to remove any excess mixture and place the fabric flat on newsprint or newspaper to drain. To speed things up, start the drying process with a warm (not hot) iron, then hang the fabric patches up to dry. When it's dry the fabric will be a dark apple green, and must then be stored in a light-proof bag. Write a label on the bag to remind you what it is, so that you don't open it up in bright sunlight and so spoil its efficacy.

The newspaper drying is fine, but don't do as I did: being conscientious about recycling, we have a newsprint collection each week. I piled all the papers in the box provided and put them out for collection. Amazingly, on that very day I thought 'where did I put all that blue print fabric?' Total horror: it was folded inside the newspapers. I had visions of chasing around the neighbourhood, finding the van and sorting through hundreds of newspapers. Luckily the delivery was an hour late that day and I was saved.

It's probably best to do all the preparation in advance of the day you hope to be printing; that way, you've got the fabric all ready as soon as the sun comes out, and don't have the added stress of 'is the sun going in?!'

Printing

Print on a day that you are sure is going to be sunny (! if you're that clever maybe you should be a weather forecaster, not a quilter ...); basically a nice clear day. A tip is to do the printing around midday, or in the late morning or early afternoon, as the intensity of the sun reduces after 3pm.

Take a piece of your prepared fabric and place it on a magazine or piece of card to make it easier to carry in and out of the house. An old clip-frame is ideal as you have the combination of a strong base and a sheet of glass. Now select your image to be printed (see the box on the left).

Put your selected object(s) on the fabric and place a piece of glass over the top if the object is likely to blow away. (Note that if you have any stray bits of threads on the fabric they will also print in the sun, so remove these carefully first.) Lay the fabric in full sun for at least 10 minutes; you'll see the fabric turn first a dark blue, then grey. The precise time the piece of fabric needs in the sun will depend on the time of day, as I've mentioned, and also where you live (the sun's rays are stronger in some areas than others).

Remove the object from the fabric and you will see the print, which is a yellow colour. Leave the fabric under running water for 20 minutes until all the chemicals have been washed from the fabric and the water runs clear. Or, fill the sink and keep on changing the rinsing water till it's clear. By this stage the fabric is blue, with a white negative image printed on it.

To enhance the colour, dip the fabric in a solution of half a teaspoonful of hydrogen peroxide to two litres of water. Rinse and dry. (Hydrogen peroxide is the stuff used for the stop bath for the bleach resists in *Quirky Quilts*, so it's probably lurking in your cupboard somewhere; if not it's available from most pharmacies.) Iron with a warm (not hot) iron, then this fascinating and original fabric is ready to be incorporated into your work.

Experimenting

I've tried all kinds of objects to create the images on the blue prints. Some of the flowers I used were dried ones. I had lent my mother-in-law a book years ago, and after she died I got it back; she used to make pressed-flower cards, and she had placed some flowers and grasses between papers in the pages. So it was a lovely way of preserving the flowers and including them in a quilt in her memory. In fact I got a very clear image from the dried flowers as some of the fresh ones under glass began to 'sweat' slightly, blurring the image.

I made my first batch of blue print fabric into *Fragments from the Sun*

The images to be sun-printed could be any of the following, or a combination:

Freshly-picked flowers, leaves or grasses

Feathers

Shells with holes in them

Lace, or doilies

Household objects: keys, toys, paperclips, combs

Sewing objects: scissors, large needles, pins, safety pins

Black and white photographic negatives (these are a bit tricky unless they are large ones)

Cut-out card or firm paper shapes

TIP

If you feel that all this messing about with chemicals is not for you, you can buy batches of fabric that are already primed for sun-printing. On page 72 you'll find details of stockists for all the different chemicals and the ready-prepared fabric.

Blue printing at a glance

1 Mix up the chemical solutions required and tip into a bowl. Cut the fabric to a handy size; working in a dark room, soak each piece in the solution, then squeeze out.

2 Lay the fabric flat on absorbent paper and leave it until it's thoroughly dry.

3 Put the fabric in a light-proof bag, clearly labelled, until it's needed.

4 On a sunny day, lay the fabric piece on a firm surface. Position your 'resist' materials (flowers, lace etc) on top of the fabric.

5 Cover the resist materials with glass and place the whole thing in the sun until the fabric has turned first blue, then grey.

6 Remove the resist materials from the fabric, then rinse the fabric thoroughly.

7 Enhance the colour by dipping the fabric into a hydrogen peroxide solution.

8 Press the fabric with a warm iron. You now have a unique fabric to incorporate into your projects.

(page 36). I couldn't decide which pieces I liked best, so I just used the lot! I then hand-quilted the quilt. The technique makes very 'livable' quilts; they have the charm of willow pattern plates. Some of my quilts are fun, but rather garish to have on permanent display in the house, but these I can live with.

The following summer I used all my needlework implements to create prints: scissors, pins, safety pins, templates, sewing machine feet, bodkins – and made *Sewing in the Sun* (detail on page 36). I added a cardboard Pimms glass with real mint as the touch of humour.

I have now discovered that if I start the process with yellow fabric I get a blue-and-yellow print. I found some yellow tie-dye fabric from many projects ago and used some of the yellow fabric left over from *Baby Talk*; to make the images I used cardboard bird shapes which were from a Danish Christmas decoration (I knew they would come in useful sometime!) and leaves, and so another quilt has been created: *A Tapestry of Birds* (see page 37).

The envelope method

I know I explained how to make quilts in this way in *Quirky Quilts*, but I think that it needs a reprise in more detail; when I'm giving talks, I often have people saying 'What a novel way of putting quilts together. How do you do it?'

I've used the envelope method in lots of my quilts, recently in *Abroad Thoughts from Home, What Shall We Call It?*, and *Baby Talk*. The advantage of this method for us bodgers is that you create your quilt in sections, which are therefore smaller to machine-quilt or to deal with under the machine if you're using other methods such as appliqué.

I know I should clear away all the detritus on my machining bench, but somehow I never do so; when I have a large quilt I'm constantly manoeuvring around all the reels of thread, fabrics, postcards, pens etc; these then all slide to the floor and get in a tangled mess, so precious time is lost in clearing up. ('My machining bench' sounds very grand; it is, in fact, the desk unit which was made out of an old kitchen worktop and used for homework when one of my sons had the room for his bedroom. I'm afraid that as they've each left home, I've quickly moved into their rooms in case they want to come back!)

Creating the blocks

With this method, each block of a quilt is made as a separate envelope; follow the instructions in the box to create your envelopes. The blocks can either be joined directly to each other (which is what I did with *They Must be Useful for Something*), or you can put sashing between them – see below.

Obviously with this method you have to measure your intended blocks carefully, otherwise they won't match up well, but if you do discover that some of your blocks are fractionally bigger or smaller than others – which usually happens to me – it doesn't matter, as you can jiggle them round to fit as you join them. I have heard this method of quilting called 'bagging it up,' which I feel is more a description of the very puffy baby quilts, made in sections, which were all the rage a few years ago.

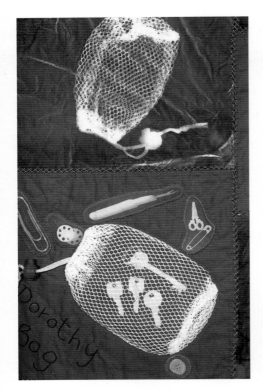

Above: detail of They Must be Useful for Something, *showing blocks joined directly with herringbone stitch*

Right: in this detail of Abroad Thoughts from Home, *you can see the herringbone stitch used to attach the sashing strips and corner blocks*

Making the blocks

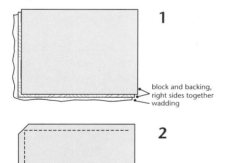

1

block and backing,
right sides together
wadding

2

3

1 Put the front of the quilt block right sides together with the back of the block, then finish off the 'sandwich' with the wadding. It seems odd having the wadding last in the sandwich, but it works out better than way.

2 Machine round three sides of the sandwich and clip across the corners; trim the wadding down to the seam line.

3 Turn the work through to the right side, fold under the raw edges on the final side and slipstitch the folded edges together.

Above: Abroad Thoughts from Home. *The luggage tags at the bottom are another good way of adding a decorative hem!*

TIP

You can use up all those odd bits of fabric that are too nice to throw away by using them as backs for your blocks or your sashing sections. Each back is fairly small, and using different fabrics creates an attractive patchwork-effect backing to the quilt as a whole.

Sashing

If you want a more traditional look for the quilt, sashing is probably called for. If you're using sashing in an envelope-method quilt, you need to make the sashing sections in the same way, but in long strips; when you've made them in long envelopes, the strips look a bit like judo belts. Follow the directions in the box to add the sashing and cover the joins at the corner blocks.

Having written all the instructions down the process of creating the envelopes and adding sashing sounds daunting, but I can assure you it isn't – and the advantage of having the smaller units to work with more than outweighs any final fiddling.

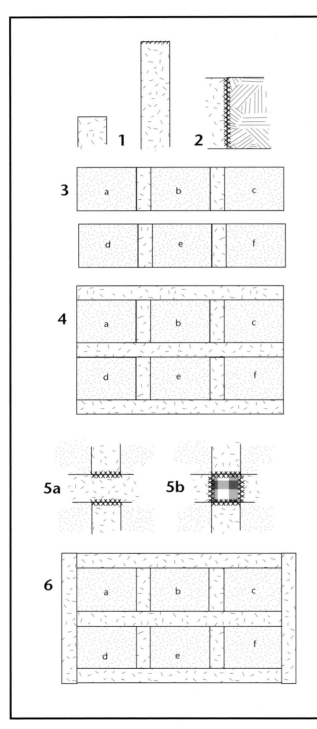

Adding sashing strips

1 To make a two-inch sashing, cut 2½-in wide strips for the front, the back and the wadding; this will give you a ¼in seam allowance on each side. Sandwich up these pieces, then stitch, turn and close just as for the blocks (see page 41).

2 Add the vertical sashes to each side of blocks b and e. ('Vertical' describes the up and down bits! It's taken me until I'm nearly 60 to get the hang of vertical and horizontal; someone recently solved it for me by saying that 'horizontal' is like the horizon.) Cut the strips to length and attach them to the blocks either with machine stitching or herringbone, as described on page 43.

3 Add blocks a and c to the outsides of block b, and blocks d and f to the outsides of block e. You now have two strips of three blocks, with two strips of sashing in each.

4 Measure the length of the strips so that you know how long to make the horizontal sashes. You will need three strips; one for the top, one for the centre, and one for the bottom. Make these and attach them in the same way as before.

5 You'll notice that where the vertical sashing strips butt up to the horizontal ones, there is a raw edge and a gap. Now some serious bodging is called for! Either paint the raw edges first with Fraycheck or dilute PVA glue, and then herringbone over the join (5a), or if they look really wonky, add a square of contrast fabric and herringbone over this to cover the evidence (5b)!

In *Why?* I used up some 'gone wrong' triangular log cabin bits to create the disguising squares. As I never throw anything away I always have something to hand which can be used in some creative way!

6 To complete the sashing, add the final vertical sashes on each end and disguise all the corners at the edges with the squares of fabric as above.

Covering the joins

The main disadvantage of this method is having to disguise the joins where the blocks meet. But, as with most of my quilts, I try to make the disadvantage into a major design feature; this can be achieved in various ways.

Fancy stitches

I find herringbone stitching a pleasing way to join the blocks. It works well as it takes a stitch from each block alternately, and can add sparkle to the surface and act as a sashing between the blocks. I use stranded embroidery cotton, halving it so that I'm working with three strands. Use a colour that's a good strong contrast to the quilt background, to give it a lift. There are other fancy stitches that work well too; experiment and see which one you like best.

The first quilt I made using this method was Why? (see *Quirky Quilts*); I herringboned the front and the back of the blocks, and it has stood the test of time well – and actually hangs straighter than most of my quilts. I now find that if you initially join the blocks with a universal stitch, which is available on lots of machines (see left) – or, at a pinch, zigzag stitch – this holds the quilt quite securely while you add the decorative stitching. As this method is very secure and joins the blocks right through from the front to the back, there's no need to add herringbone on the back unless you want to. If you really want to disguise the fact that the quilt is made in portions, have a very 'busy' print on the back and using a toning thread for the joining stitches.

Bonded shapes

You can also cover the joins between blocks by bonding shapes cut out from printed fabric; I did this with *Baby Talk*. I dyed the fabric yellow for this quilt with a washing-machine dye. (If you haven't tried this, do have a go; the washing machine doesn't stain, it makes a really even dye for a large amount of fabric, and you can always chuck in those faded undies to give them a lift!) The colour made the quilt very cheerful, but it still needed something to accentuate the different blocks.

I had some children's curtain fabric (I really can't remember why I bought it; probably it was in a sale ...) It featured teddy bears and letters in bright colours on a white background. I ironed Bondaweb on the back of the motifs, then cut them out and fused them in place in strips on the quilt top. As I always worry that Bondaweb won't withstand the wear and tear my quilts get, I stitched around each motif. (When I give quilt talks I usually take bags of quilts and people really like to handle them; therefore I always like to stitch fabrics as well as bond them.) The stitching is a buttonhole-type stitch which my machine does; it's called edging stitch. I realised that, rather than trying to stitch round each motif individually, it was much easier to stitch down one side of the whole line (a) and then up the other (b) – especially as now the quilt was quite big and stuff was being pushed off my workbench onto the floor!

You could try this method with any printed motifs; flowers, leaves and patterned strips of fabric would all make effective joining strips.

I use this universal stitch (number 6 on the Bernina) for holding the blocks together while I add the decorative stitching. If your machine doesn't have this stitch, try a zigzag

a   b

TIP

Read the instructions on the Bondaweb; it actually requires using a damp cloth to make the bond as effective as possible.

TIME-SAVING TIPS

If I could have a pound for every time I'm asked 'How ever do you get time to do all this quilting?', I'd be a tax exile living on a far-off island. In this section you'll find some of my time-saving ideas; some of them are a bit of a cheat, but some are just based on common sense!

One of the secrets, though, is not being a perfectionist; as I mentioned before, life's too short to fret about every tiny blemish on a quilt, or to give up on a project just because it hasn't gone totally according to plan … I actually started quilting professionally because of a minor disaster. John was made redundant from a large architectural practice in his fifties, so we decided to start our own practice from home. This meant that I gave up adult craft teaching, learnt computer skills and had more time to pursue my own quilting, as I was tied to the house/office and the phone.

The extra time I then put in quilting led in turn to me being asked to demonstrate and give lectures; as we were self-employed we could both take time to travel to talks during the week and then catch up with office work on wet weekends. So the seeming disaster of the loss of a job turned into opportunities I never dreamed of.

Your individual circumstances will be different from mine, but there are still lots of ways in which you can streamline your time to create precious quilting time. As every quilter with a family knows, it can be difficult balancing the conflicting demands of work, family, housework and quilting. Obviously if your family is sympathetic to your hobby, that helps! I think my quilt *Who Would Marry a Quilter?* was inspired by families I've seen while I've been demonstrating at shows; watching poor men being dragged along, pretending to show interest, is somewhat amusing – but how thrilled would you be at a computer show? I have three sons and have been to more army and war museums than I care to remember.

At shows I always try to have things people can touch, and this goes down well with children, who are being browbeaten not to touch at every turn and often must wish they'd opted to stay at home. If we don't encourage the young quilters, when all we grannies have gone who will carry on the good work? It's great if we can get our children and grandchildren involved in our own work. Another way of creating more sewing time for yourself is to sit down and do things together – then your children won't be begging you to take them to the swimming pool or the computer games shop instead! Whatever your family circumstances, though, try out some of these time-saving tips and tricks.

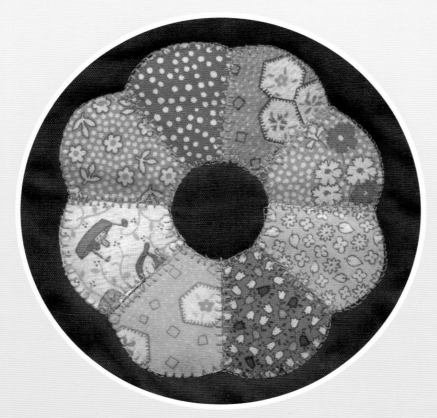

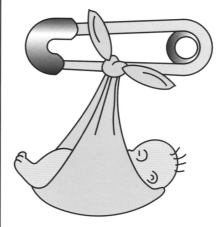

Quick cathedral window

is really back to the very beginning for me, as it was the pattern which intrigued me so much that I joined a class to learn how to quilt. This easy version is an accurate way of stitching the pattern by hand.

Cheaty baby quilts

On these pages I show you how to make a couple of very quick and easy baby quilts based on my own quilt *Baby Talk*.

Opposite: make cathedral window cushions in no time at all!

Above: detail of the Dresden Plate quilt, one of two cheaty baby quilts based on my own piece Baby Talk

Below: both quick-and-easy baby quilts, modelled by Constance

Making time for quilting

is packed with different ways I save time in other areas so that I can get on with my stitching – maybe you could try a couple of the ideas?

Fast food

There's a myth that quilters don't cook. I certainly do, and here I share some of my delicious quick-and-easy recipes. Honestly, the family

will be so happy with some home-cooked food that they'll forgive all that sewing mess around the house!

Quick cathedral window

Cathedral window was the reason I first joined a patchwork class, and met my very best friend (embroiderer Linda Tudor), and became a professional patchworker – so it's quite a block! Linda and I went to an exhibition at the local Adult Institute and saw this wonderful design in a sampler quilt; it was three-dimensional, and really intriguing.

We joined the class and learned how to make the block; we then joined forces in a stall in Covent Garden Market, which led to us making cathedral window cushions for major London stores. We found that using a cardboard template made the windows more

Cathedral window cushion cover

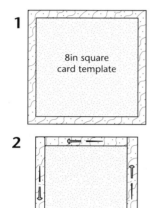

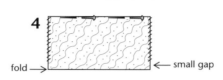

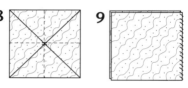

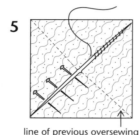

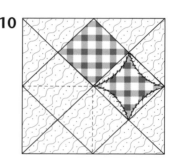

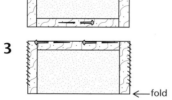

1   Cut an 8in (20cm) square template from thin card (an old cereal packet works well): this is your template. Cut four pieces of plain coloured fabric 8½in (22.5cm) square. Lay one of the patches right side down on a flat surface, and position the template in the centre.

2   Fold the edges of the square over the edges of the card and pin them in position, pulling the fabric taut across the card shape.

3   Fold the card shape in half so that the fabric is inside, and oversew the two short sides from the top down to within ¼in (5mm) of the folded edge.

4   Move the pins to mark the folded edges of the fabric along the top edges (not pinning through the card this time). Remove the card template, and turn the rectangle right side out.

5   Pull the unstitched edges outwards and fold them so that you form a square shape with a long slit down the centre as shown; pin the edges of this slit together, then oversew them. This sewing will all be covered, so you don't need to be too worried about it being neat!

6   Make sure you leave small gaps (about ¼in) at the ends of the oversewn edges as shown; these create a much neater square with really crisp corners when the shapes are turned out.

7   Fold two corners of the new square to the centre as shown and secure them with a couple of small stitches.

8   Fold in the other two corners and secure them in the same way. Repeat all the steps with the remaining three squares so that you now have four complete units.

9   Lay two units folded sides together and oversew them down one edge to join them. Use the same method to create a block of four units in a square.

accurate, and they could be sewn entirely by hand; it's the same old trick that, if you can hand-sew it, you can be more productive as any odd moments can be used for sewing. We made kits and sold them on our market stall, and devised a method so that only four 'windows' are needed to cover a 12in cushion (see the examples on page 48). Now there's a timesaver! The same four basic units can also be used to produce a sewing bag or a glasses case instead (see pages 49-50).

Pure cotton fabric works best for making the main units; calico is a traditional choice, and works well contrasted with country prints etc, but you can use any plain colour or any small overall pattern or print. Avoid large patterns and strong prints, otherwise the pattern will become hopelessly confused when you've done all the folding.

10 Cut four 2in (5cm) squares from a contrast fabric and position them over the stitched background as shown. Roll the folded edges over the sides of the contrast squares (these roll over very satisfyingly as the folds are all on the bias) and slipstitch them in position to anchor the inserted patches. Leave a scant ¼in (about 3mm) unstitched at the ends of the curved edges. This stitching does show, so you need to be a bit neater ...

11 Cut eight 4in (10cm) squares from a third fabric and position them round the central unit as shown.

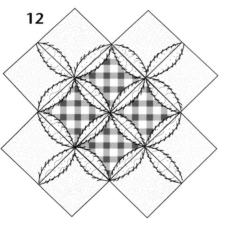

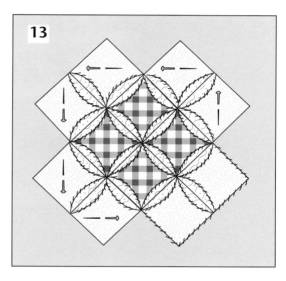

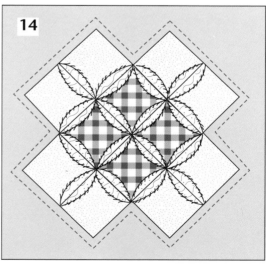

12 Roll back two edges of the basic units to trap two sides of each new fabric square as shown; slipstitch each of these in place.

13 Cut a 12½in (35cm) square of background fabric for your cushion cover, and a piece of wadding the same size. Pin the patchwork piece

in the centre of the background fabric. Turn under and pin the raw edges around the shape, then slipstitch them in position.

14 Lay the background square over the wadding and quilt round the edges of the shape; hold down the

centre of each flower shape with small stitches. Make up the cushion cover as described in the *Basic Boring Bits* (page 69).

Choose contrasting colours for the inserted squares – you can use cotton again in a different colour or a strong pattern, or pick silk or some other exotic fabric that stands out well. Try out both dark and light background colours; brightly-patterned inserted squares look wonderful against silk or cotton in rich jewel colours, and also against plain black or navy blue.

When you're securing the rolled-over edges, make sure that you stitch right through all the layers each time. The reason for doing this is that it's a very tactile pattern, with lots of heavy textures, and people are always trying to work out how it's done. They can't resist poking their fingers underneath the folds; if you stitch all the way through the layers, though, they can't!

TIP

Remember to leave the tiny gaps at each end of your oversewing lines when you're creating the foundation blocks for cathedral window; they help create really crisp corners when you turn the shapes out.

If they still look a bit sorry for themselves, poke them out into crisp shapes using the tip of your scissors or (gently) the point of a seam ripper.

Opposite page: several cushion covers in different colour-schemes, all decorated with cathedral window blocks as described on page 46-47

Above: Four cathedral window blocks can be combined to create a padded glasses case, or a little bag for your hand-sewing; see the instructions on page 50

Left: cathedral window blocks at various stages of assembly

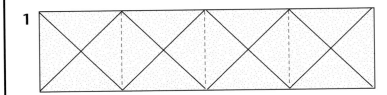

1

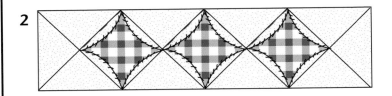

2

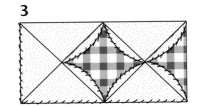

3

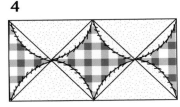

4

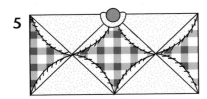

5

Simple sewing bag

1 Follow the steps for making a cushion up to step 8 (see page 46); you now have the basic four units. Stitch them all in a row as shown.

2 Add the contrast fabric inserts, rolling over the folded edges and slipstitching them as before.

3 Fold the row in half and oversew down the side and along the bottom to create a bag shape.

4 Add a final square of contrast fabric over the stitched edge to cover the side join, rolling over the folded edges and stitching them as before.

5 Sew a loop and button or velcro patches at the top and you have a little bag, already lined and padded – perfect for carrying around little bits of hand-sewing.

You could make a larger bag with two rows of six blocks in exotic fabrics, and use it as an evening bag.

Jazzy glasses case

1

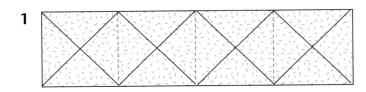

2 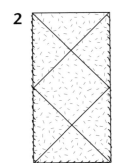 3  4

1 Follow the steps for making a cushion up to step 8 (see page 46), but using a 6in (15cm) square template to begin with. If you're making a case for sunglasses, you could use bright cotton for the foundation squares and jazzy fabrics as your contrast pieces. (You could also pad each of the squares with a square of wadding at stage 5 to give the sewing a more sculptured look.) You now have the basic four units.

2 Stitch them all in a row, then fold the row in half and stitch it down the edges and bottom as shown.

3 Add the contrast squares as before, rolling over the edges and slipstitching them.

4 Add a couple of velcro patches at the top of the case to stop your glasses slipping out.

Cheaty baby quilts

It's nice to make a small cot quilt for a new baby, but inevitably time is always at a premium. If it's a grandchild you'll probably be asked either to look after the existing children, or to cook meals and generally be on hand rather than sitting filling your days with delicate hand-sewing ...

These days girls are lucky to stay in hospital for more than 24 hours, and grannies are a very useful help. Therefore the last thing on your mind is likely to be making a time-consuming quilt. Or, if it's your own baby, you'll have lots of other things to think about. I always feel like persuading pregnant girls to go out a lot as it's a darn site easier to take the baby out *in utero* than arranging babysitters once it's here.

To create a quick quilt for a baby, you could just machine-quilt round a printed panel, but these two quilts are quick and easy options and look as if you've spent ages making them! You could of course be like a lady in my quilt group: each time there was a show and tell she would bring a beautiful cot quilt. One day someone asked however many grandchildren she had. The answer was, none: she was pre-making them so that when eventually they arrived she would have more time for more important things like hugging them and playing with them.

My quilt *Baby Talk* (see page 52) is made up of six miniature quilts; you'll find details of them on page 53. Two of these designs I've made larger so that you can make them up into full-size baby quilts. The secret behind both of these is the ubiquitous Bondweb. I know it makes the fabric stiff, but it washes well and is very easy to use; also, you can now sometimes get other, softer bonding webs. (As I mentioned before, do read the manufacturer's instructions in order to get a good bond.)

Using the Bondaweb means that all the raw edges of the fabric shapes are bonded to the background fabric and so won't fray; that in turn means that you don't need to add any seam allowance, or do any piecing. The patches for each design are just cut to shape, then fused in position on the background – like a kind of marquetry in fabric. To make the edges extra-secure, and to add decoration, I've then gone over the joins and edges with a decorative machine stitch; this also quilts the designs at the same time.

Each set of instructions is for a crib or small pram quilt, which is smaller than a drop-side cot quilt. The average size of a cot mattress is 22x45in (55x115cm); if you want a quilt that will tuck in or hang over the mattress, you'll need to make it about 24x48in (60x120cm). So, if you want to enlarge the pram quilt designs here, either make a larger border or add an extra row of Dresden Plates or Tumbling Blocks. I've made my baby quilts in dark background colours so that they don't show the dirt (!), but they could both be made in lighter colours if you prefer.

TIP

To find the relative tones of fabric, try using a door spy (see page 10); these give the impression that the work is in the distance, and the tones show up more clearly. You can also use a child's telescope (available extremely cheaply from the Early Learning Centre), using it the wrong way round to reduce what you're seeing.

Another method is to stick a small strip of each fabric onto a sheet of white paper and then photocopy it using a black and white copier; the relative tones will then be obvious. An even quicker way is to put all the fabrics near each other and then half-close your eyes and squint at them, which shows the tones up quite well.

Above: **Baby Talk**

Opposite, top; details of the miniature quilts from the carrycots on **Baby Talk**

Opposite, below; the two full-size Bondawebbed baby quilts, modelled with Constance (named after the embroiderer Constance Howard, who always dyed her hair bright green!)

Easy Dresden Plate quilt

Apparently this pattern was popular in the 1930s, when people couldn't afford real china; instead, they created the pattern of the plates in patchwork for wedding quilts. For this design, I used a small Dresden Plate design from Angela Besley's book *Rose Windows for Quilters* (see page 72).

MATERIALS

- *Twelve different small-print fabrics, one 5in (13cm) square of each*
- *Twelve 5in (13cm) squares of double-sided bonding web*
- *Plain background fabric, 20x26in (50x65cm)*
- *Backing fabric, 20x26in (50x65cm)*
- *2oz wadding, 20x26in (50x65cm)*
- *Paper and pencil*
- *For marking the background fabric: hardened soap or pale crayon if the fabric is dark, or a soft pencil if the fabric is pale*
- *Thin card and glue, or template plastic*

METHOD

1 Trace the pattern on page 54 onto tracing paper, or photocopy it. Stick the pattern onto thin card and cut it out to create a template, or cut the shape from the template plastic.

2 Place one square of Bondaweb, rough side down, on the wrong side of each print fabric square; press with a warm iron to fuse the Bondaweb in place.

3 Lay the template on the paper side of each square and trace round the outside edge and the inside circle. Join the indents (shown as dotted lines on the template) with a ruler to divide each shape into twelve sections.

4 Leaving a 1in (2.5cm) border all round the edges, mark your plain background fabric into 6in (15cm) squares – you'll have three squares across and four down.

5 Peel away the backing papers from the plate shapes, then cut each plate into eight sections along the straight lines.

6 Lay the template in the centre of each marked square and draw round the outside edge; this gives you a positioning guide for the plate sections.

7 Mix up the coloured segments so that each new plate has a good assortment and arrangement of segments, then position the plates inside the drawn plate shapes, web side down. Iron all the shapes to bond them in position. When you're bonding, work on one square at a time so that you don't knock any bits out of position.

8 Lay the backing fabric on a flat surface and cover it with the wadding; lay the Dresden Plate piece, right side up, on top of the wadding and pin/safety-pin or tack the three layers together – whichever method you prefer.

9 Cover the long straight lines (the ones marking off the edges of the squares) with a fancy stitch on your machine, working in a contrasting colour. (If you don't have any fancy stitches, a large zigzag would do fine.) I used a straight stitch in yellow to show up against the dark blue background, then worked down each side of the straight stitch in No13 on my Bernina. This could be an opportunity to use all those stitches you thought would be so useful when you bought the machine, but haven't so far done anything with! Alternatively, you could sew lengths of fancy ribbon or coloured tape over the lines.

10 Cover the joins on the plates with a fancy stitch on your machine (I used my machine's stitch No21, which is an imitation buttonhole-stitch), or with zigzag; then go round the inside and outside edges of each plate shape with the same stitch. This quilts the plates and secures them in position.

11 To finish the edges, fold the top fabric back against the stitched line. Use a rotary cutter to cut the wadding and backing to ½in (12mm) outside the stitched line round each edge; make sure that you keep the top fabric out of the way of the rotary cutter. Fold the top fabric to the back in a small double hem and stitch it in place by hand or machine.

Don't forget to sign the quilt and dedicate it to the baby!

TIP

Template plastic is very useful for making your own templates; it's cheap and durable, and you can use it over and over again. For these designs lay the plastic over the pattern piece and trace the line in pencil; cut out the template with paper scissors – and remember to write on it what design it's for.

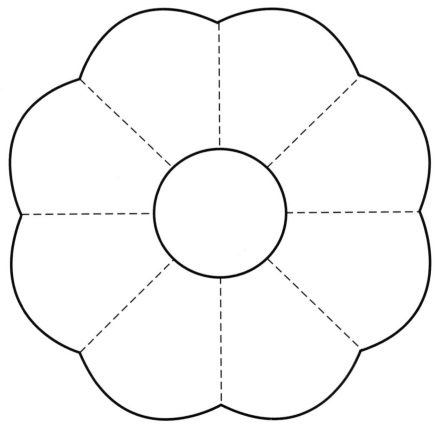

Quick Tumbling Blocks

Did you know that this pattern is on a piazza at Pompeii? So there's nothing new under the sun. This pattern of diamonds arranged to give the effect of three-dimensional blocks is usually stitched using the English method of patchwork, pieced over papers; by bonding the diamonds it speeds things up considerably. To make the pattern work you need to have light, medium and dark-toned fabrics.

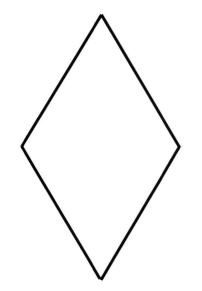

MATERIALS

- *Three small-print fabrics; light, medium and dark in tone (I actually used two different medium-toned fabrics, and two different dark-toned ones, just for variety)*

- *Plain background fabric, 26x37in (66x94cm) (remember to choose a contrast to your block fabrics, otherwise they won't show up)*

- *Backing fabric, 26x37in (66x94cm)*

- *2oz wadding, 26x37in (66x94cm)*

- *Bondaweb*

- *Paper and pencil*

- *Chalk marker or hard soap*

- *Thin card and glue, or template plastic*

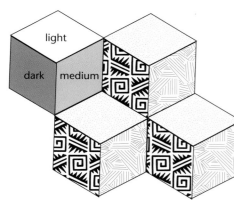

1 Trace the diamond shape (above left) onto tracing paper, or photocopy it. Stick the pattern onto thin card and cut it out to create a template, or cut the shape from the template plastic.

2 Iron bonding web onto the back of each print fabric piece.

3 On the paper side of the bonding web, draw repeats of the diamond template (you will need 55 light, 55 medium and 55 dark). Cut out all the diamonds along the drawn lines.

4 On your foundation fabric, draw a border 2in (5cm) in from each edge, using either a chalk marker or hard soap.

5 Peel the backing papers away from the diamond shapes and place them on the foundation fabric, within the marked border, following the layout shown (left). Iron the diamonds in place, using a damp cloth, to fuse them to the background.

6 Lay the backing fabric, right side down, on a flat surface and position the wadding on top; cover the wadding with the Tumbling Blocks design, right side up. Pin or tack the three layers together.

7 Stitch around each diamond shape with a fancy stitch on your machine, or use zigzag stitch. This decorative stitching disguises any mismatches and quilts the three layers together in one action. What a time-saver! Stitch an outside border in the same stitch, or echo the outlines of the Tumbling Blocks design.

8 Follow the instructions for the Dresden Plate quilt to trim and hem the edges, or bind them with strips of toning fabric.

9 Make a label and sew it to the back of the quilt with the baby's name and date of birth – and, of course, lots of love from you.

> ### TIP
>
> *To vary the pattern, add a circle of yellow fabric over the middle of the Dresden Plate shape; it creates the effect of a flower.*

Right: in this detail of the Dresden Plate quilt, you can see the decorative stitching that I've worked round squares, in yellow, and the machine 'blanket-stitch' round the patches making up the plate.

Below: detail of the Tumbling Blocks quilt, showing the fancy machine stitch worked between the diamonds

You could use any traditional block or repeat pattern with this method, or try simple appliqué motifs; the designs shown here would all work well. Just trace around the individual segments, cut and bond them to the backing, then disguise the joins with stitchery. It's not cheating: it's a new method of patchwork called Fabric Marquetry ...

Making time for quilting

How do you make more time for quilting, and still keep the family happy? Now there's a challenge! The most frequently asked question when I give a talk is *How do you get time to do all these quilts?* That is, after they've said *Has anyone told you that you look just like Delia Smith?!* (The cookery guru, for anyone who doesn't know.) At this stage I have to point out that patchwork and quilting is my job. I'm lucky: I don't have to juggle my obsession with another paid job. I get paid for doing what I love, sharing my quilts with people and making them laugh!

I happen to make quite a few quilts a year, but that's my choice; I use quilting as a sort of Valium tranquilliser – it's the thing that keeps me sane. I'm sure if the government did studies they would find that quilters are less stressed than the rest of the female population 'of a certain age.' That's because it's such a sharing and caring hobby; there are so many troubles and disasters that can be discussed and sorted whilst stitching. Somehow, while they're sewing people feel freer to discuss their worries than if they're sitting face to face with nothing to keep their hands occupied. In fact we should all demand free prescriptions for our sewing needs; we're saving the National Health Service a fortune. The other wonderful thing is that quilters come in all shapes, sorts, sizes and ages; the older ones can give their advice from years of experience, and the younger ones can keep the older ones up to date.

Here are some tips for making more time to quilt:

Have a deadline

This can either be an exhibition, or a special occasion such as a birthday or wedding for which you're making the quilt. (A personalised cushion is a lovely and welcome wedding present if you feel that a quilt is somewhat over the top!) It's amazing how you can speed up when the deadline is looming. If you have never entered an exhibition, be brave and remember we all were virgin exhibitors at some time. If you enter an all-comers show first you can be confident that your quilt will be hung; when you get a bit braver, enter the juried exhibitions. Even then, if your quilt isn't accepted, don't walk about doom-laden – tell your quilting friends; they'll probably then admit that theirs wasn't chosen either. I know some quilts which were refused in one exhibition and won a first prize in another.

My reason for entering exhibitions is to get work finished; also I sometimes find that if there is a subject it can encourage me to make a quilt on a topic that I'd never have thought of – pregnancy for instance! If you win a rosette, that's lovely, but it's not the object of the exercise. I once mentioned to one of my sons that my quilt had won a prize at a show. He was horrified that I had won a rosette, and not a car or lots of money! I'm very happy that cash prizes haven't hit Britain in a big way as yet. The rosette is recognition that your quilting peers felt the quilt deserves praise for its design and workmanship.

Have lots of projects on the go

It's not a race (unless it's for an exhibition, see above!), so if you have a 'life's work' on the go, as I did with *Just in Case of Hijack*, it doesn't matter how many years it takes; it can be a sewing project for those times when you can't think of anything new. This is why I like projects that can be built up in sections or blocks. They can be transported around with you, and it's really amazing how much you can get done in odd moments while waiting for trains, planes, appointments.

This means you don't get as much reading done, but you could have the ultimate experience: read and sew at the same time with talking book tapes. My father was blind in his old age and admitted that through talking books he 'read' more books than he ever did when he was sighted. My ultimate Saturday afternoon is a really good play on the radio and some patchwork. (Isn't that sad? I really should get out more!)

Make up kits

These can contain all the cut fabric ready for piecing, or blocks marked for quilting. Bag them up and even put in the thread and needle. When you have a spare moment and think 'It's not worth trying to get something prepared to sew,' it's all ready for you. These kits can be invaluable for journeys or waiting rooms. When the plane is delayed once again, you can be the only person with a broad smile.

By having hand- and machine-sewing in progress it means you can machine in the day and hand-sew at night, so that you don't exclude yourself from the family – although then you have to rely on them telling you who is who on the TV as you're only listening.

Have a sewing room or area

This is a luxury, but if you have a spare bedroom, think how many times you actually have guests and consider turning it into a sewing room. You can buy specially designed cupboards to house all your fabric, machine, cutting gear, and even include a lightbox. It all folds away and looks like a piece of furniture, so it could be used in any room in the house. These desks are expensive, but not as expensive as building on a sewing room/studio.

I heard a lovely story at a talk I was giving last year. In the show and tell a lady showed a scrap quilt which she said had cost her £20,000. She had made it for her spare room single bed. It turned out to be a double quilt, so they bought a double bed; this wouldn't fit in the room, so they had to build a loft extension – hence the cost! Your guests will be interested to sleep in a room which contains your quilting books, fabrics and design sheets, and if they don't they can go to a local B&B in future. You'll be amazed at how productivity goes up if you don't have to clear everything off the kitchen/dining room table each time a meal is ready.

Another speeding-up boon is a design wall. This sounds very grand, but I pin some lengths of curtain interfacing (the man-made sort) to the wall; this is fluffy and has a slightly sticky effect on the fabric, so pieces stay put when they're placed on it like children's Fuzzy Felt

TIP

For hand-sewing/quilting I wear a magnifying glass suspended on a string round my neck; you can obtain them from needlework shops or opticians. This makes the stitches appear large, and then magically when you look without the glass they are very small and neat. The glass will fall down if you don't sit up straight (unless you have a very voluptuous bust!), and as you aren't slouching over your work it avoids pains in the neck and shoulders.

A major advantage of this method is that it strengthens your eye muscles, therefore improving your eyesight! As you look at the sewing your eyes are focusing for near sight, then as you glance up at the TV every few seconds the muscles are refocusing for long sight. I only very occasionally use very weak reading glasses and I use my eyes all day – and I'm nearly 60. Now if I could remember to flex my stomach muscles at the same time that really would be an advantage …

figures. You can look at your design from a distance and move blocks around before sewing. If you're spatially challenged like me, and have forgotten which bit goes where by the time you get it to the machine, a good idea is to pin a paper number onto each piece and stitch them in sequence.

If you live alone, maybe you can just let the quilting take over the whole house, but however obsessed we are with our quilts there are other things to do in life. Don't feel guilty about having a room for your hobby; if your husband is a golfer you wouldn't expect him to play in the back garden. He needs a proper place to carry out his hobby, and so do you. A quilter I met many years ago was a widow and a fanatical quilter; she decided not to waste time cooking or washing up. She had one cup for tea and one for coffee, which could be rinsed or not. She ate sandwiches for two days, then went to the pub for some hot food on the third day, and was as happy as Larry. (I'll tell you how you can cook and quilt on page 63.)

Dedicate a day a week for your quilting (or more!)

Pencil in a day a week in your diary and make that your quilting day; ask a friend round so that you can't decide to skip it and go shopping instead. I know of people who attend a class regularly for years just so they get a quilting day a week. You could pretend to go to a class, then tell your friends and family that you're out every Tuesday so not to call or ring … You can then have a lovely day sewing and listening to the radio, and get so much sewing done. My friends still think I work more or less full-time doing John's typing; I haven't told them that he now does most of it himself and that my quilting output has therefore gone up considerably.

I had the same idea about Christmas; so many friends say they wish they didn't always have to have the family round, but don't want to be away from home. I suggest that they pretend to be away and then hide at home. My other silly suggestion for making Christmas more agreeable is Swap A Granny For Christmas. Have you noticed how other people's parents are so much more interesting than your own, as you haven't heard their 'fascinating' stories twenty times?

Have quilting time

Is there a dead time of day when you're sitting twiddling your thumbs, which could be quilting time? Maybe you could get up an hour earlier each day (or maybe not; if you're like me, it's far more appealing to roll over and go back to sleep). I do find that a lot of my planning time is in the middle of the night. I get my best ideas for quilts and projects when I'm lying awake in the small hours. You could plan your quilts while waiting in queues at shop checkouts and other 'dead' time. It may be getting a bit obsessive if you're reduced to drawing out blocks on the back of till receipts, but I have known people who do this.

Delegate

I know we all think we can do a job better than anyone else, but the more you do, the more you'll be asked to do. If there are 120 women in your quilt group, take stock and think 'Why have I been on the committee three times?' Give someone else a turn. They'll say they have no time etc etc, the same old story, but learn to ask people to do things in such a nice and jokey way that they find they've offered and can't take it back.

The same applies to your household: if you iron clothes for your grown-up children they'll never leave home! Any child over 10 can iron without danger, and they have learnt a life skill. I gave up one day when I'd ironed the sixteenth shirt on the trot, and made a rule that all the boys ironed their own shirts. This did backfire slightly as they only ironed the one they wanted to wear, leaving a mountainous washing basket.

If you are under 40 your partner, if you have one, will be a 'new man' and naturally help with household chores and cooking. If you are over this age and your husband retires it can create a danger zone; I've seen many people tear their hair out, saying 'I married him for better or worse, but not for lunch!' If you're in this situation, have a complete re-think of the division of labour. If he's going out to golf or fishing and expects a meal on return, suggest that when you come back from quilting you expect the same.

Mind you, if you are feeling hard done by, take stock: could you actually mend the fuse and change the car tyre? If the answer is no, maybe you should learn. My father made me change a tyre when I was 18. It was after my mother had died, and he and I were going to a family party; I was driving and was wearing a green voile dress. The steering felt all strange and he said we had a puncture. He told me that if I changed the wheel he would tell me what to do, so that if it happened again I could deal with it. Like a mug I did as I was told, jacking up the car and messing around with all the dirt in my party dress while he kept clean and directed operations.

The next time I had a puncture I was wearing a white wool coat, so thought I wouldn't repeat the previous experience; I put on some sunglasses (to make myself look younger!) and stood by the car looking pathetic. A man stopped and changed the wheel for me quicker than a racing pit stop, but I did have the satisfaction of knowing I could do it if necessary.

These things only apply if you aren't living alone. If you do live on your own, you can probably suit yourself as to how you arrange your daily timetable. Have you thought of having a monthly lunch club? A widowed neighbour of mine did this and it worked really well. Once a month you cook a roast dinner with all the trimmings for three friends, then on the other three Sundays you get invited out for a nice dinner without the washing up! If you do live alone and long for company you could offer to be the lady in the quilt group who hosts the visiting speakers. I have had many a convivial meal or night's stays with delightful ladies who live alone. (Well, I enjoyed it, and I hope they did.)

Keep them happy

I have found after 37 years of marriage that the old saying 'The way to a man's heart is through his stomach' is true. This in fact goes for the entire family. I shall probably get hate mail from lots of quilters when I admit that next to quilting my passion is food and cooking. When I demonstrate at shows and exhibitions and John, my husband, is nobly standing beside me helping, people always come up to him and say 'You poor thing; I expect you never get a square meal with all this quilting.' (This was the idea that sparked my quilt *Who Would Marry a Quilter,* see page 13.)

I'm slapdash about many things: housework, clearing up, hanging my clothes up – but meals are something I organise like a military manoeuvre. I make a list at the beginning of each week of each day's supper/dinner. I check with the diary, so that I know which evenings we'll need to be out early and therefore require a speedy meal. (I even plan that if I'm teaching I don't want to fry onions just beforehand so that the classroom doesn't smell like a burger bar.) Then when I go shopping I can make sure I have the entire week's ingredients. This all means that when I'm tired at the end of the day I'm not in a panic as to what's for supper: it's all planned out.

Here are some tips to keep them happy, and starting opposite you'll find some mouth-watering recipes; most are quick and simple, but if you're a little inventive (as with quilting), you can make something simple or which has come out of a tin appear as if it's cordon bleu!

- Lay the table and give him a drink; it creates the feeling that supper is imminent even if it's not.

- Make your family sit down together and eat at the table at least a few times a week. I know in these days of hurry hurry this isn't always possible, but I always told my family that the evening meal wasn't a re-fuelling stop, it was when we sat and talked as a family. I fear that the whole nation will soon be sitting eating in front of TV, and dining tables will be in museums.

- Garnish food with herbs etc; it always looks as if you've spent hours in the kitchen.

- Have your music/CD player in the kitchen; it makes cooking such a pleasure, with some calming music instead of the gloomy news on the radio. Many people have TV in the kitchen, but I can never understand how they cook and watch at the same time.

- Remember that the fastest food is something like an omelette; you can have it made in the time it would have taken backing the car out to go to the takeaway.

Fast Food

These are recipes given to me by friends; I always use their names so that when I cook that particular recipe it reminds me of happy meals with them in the past. The recipes are mostly very simple and 'cheaty', but if you're determined to hate home cooking skip this bit and carry on reading on page 69 ...

Starters

- ## Leo's Chicken Liver Pate

  8oz tub of frozen chicken livers   *4oz butter*
  clove of garlic   *a sherry-glass-full of sherry*

Defrost the chicken livers and fry them gently in melted butter with the crushed garlic; when just turning brown but not burnt, add the sherry. When cool, liquidise, and leave to set either in individual dishes or one dish. Will freeze.

- ## Kipper Pate

  1 tin kippers (works better than fresh: no bones!)
  1 tub cream cheese
  1 teaspoonful lemon zest

Liquidise the cheese and the kippers, adding the lemon zest plus salt and pepper; add some fresh lemon juice if it's too stiff. Refrigerate. Serve with wedges of lemon and thin toast, and keep mum when they ask for the recipe.

- ## Avocado En Croute

  avocado pears   *tin of crabmeat*
  mayonnaise   *puff pastry*

Either halve or quarter the avocados (depending on whether main course or starter), then fill the cavity with crabmeat mixed with mayonnaise. Wrap the avocado pieces in puff pastry and bake them in a hot oven. Very filling as a starter.

Main Meals

- ## Easy Coronation Chicken

  cooked chicken
  curry paste
  toasted almond flakes

  jar of mayonnaise
  green grapes or a tin of lychees

  Add the curry paste to the mayonnaise to taste, and coat the chicken. Add the grapes or lychees and sprinkle with toasted almonds.

- ## John's Mum's Quick Grilled Fish

  fillets of cod or haddock, either fresh, or frozen and defrosted
  Heinz salad dressing or similar (yes, that disgusting-looking yellow stuff)
  chopped chives to garnish

  Cover the grill pan with tin foil (or the sauce will drip through and get lost!), then heat the grill to maximum. Cover the fish fillets with the salad cream and sprinkle with chives; grill for about six minutes, or until the salad cream has turned into a delicious sauce with a slightly brown top and the fish is cooked when you poke it with a skewer.

- ## Savoury Pancakes

  Pancakes

  4oz plain flour
  ½ pint milk

  1 egg
  salt

  Put all the ingredients in the liquidiser and whisk them until smooth; cook the pancakes in a small pan. (They can be cooked in advance and frozen, then taken out when you need them.)

  Fillings

  tin of condensed celery soup and a tin of tuna
  leftover chicken in white sauce
  any leftover casserole to make it go further
  spinach and bacon

- ## Pork Casserole

  1lb of diced pork
  tin of ratatouille
  glass of red wine
  4 sticks celery
  seasoned flour

  tin of tomatoes
  8oz mushrooms
  mixed herbs
  olive oil
  2 bay leaves

Put some flour, mixed herbs, and salt and pepper in a plastic bag; put the pork in the bag and shake until it's coated lightly with the flour. In a wok, fry the pork in batches in the olive oil till it's sealed and slightly brown. Put the meat in a casserole and add the tomatoes, ratatouille, chopped mushrooms, chopped celery and bay leaves; add the wine and a little water if needed. Cook in a medium oven for two hours.

This is better made the day before and reheated; chicken pieces can be used instead of pork.

- ### Liver

To make this more palatable and seem nicer, get the frozen lambs' liver and slice it very thinly while it's still semi frozen; fry some thin onion rings and then fry the liver till just brown. Put it on a plate to keep warm, then add a glass of sherry to the pan and scrape up the burnt bits; add some gravy granules and a little potato water, and it makes such a nice gravy you forget that it's liver! Serve with grilled bacon and mashed potatoes. You can feed three people for about 50 pence.

- ### Pork Chops With Apples

4 pork chops	*2 Cox's apples*
apple juice or brandy	*creme fraiche*

Heat a little olive oil in a frying pan and when it's very hot quickly brown the chops each side. If you're using brandy, turn down the heat slightly, pour in a little brandy and set alight!! (Beware big flames.) Immediately put on a lid to staunch the flames. If you're using apple juice pour a wine-glass-full on top of the chops. Then cover and simmer for 6-10 minutes –- until no blood comes out when a sharp knife is inserted. Take the chops out and keep them warm; add two tablespoons of creme fraiche and stir in with the burnt bits and juices to make a sauce. Meanwhile fry the slices of apple (unpeeled) in a little butter and serve with the chops. Makes pork chops very tender.

- ### John's Pork Aux Pruneaux!!

2oz raisins	*4 sage leaves*
tin of prunes, strained and de-stoned	*salt & pepper*

Liquidise all the above ingredients. Unstring a joint of pork and spread it with the mixture; tie it up and re-weigh it, and cook for 25 minutes per pound in a hot oven.

VEGETARIAN DISHES

- ### Aubergine Bake

3 slices brown bread made into breadcrumbs	
1 aubergine cut in strips lengthways	*one onion, chopped*
clove of garlic	*tin of tomatoes*
1oz or a sprinkling of pine kernels	*mixed herbs*
2oz grated cheese	*olive oil*

Brush the aubergines with olive oil and grill them on both sides till brown. Layer the tomatoes, onions and aubergines in an ovenproof dish, spreading each layer with herbs. Finally sprinkle the pine kernels over and top with the breadcrumbs mixed with the cheese. Bake in a medium oven for half an hour or until brown and crunchy on top. For variations add bacon and mushrooms, or just mushrooms.

- ### Braised Fennel

Trim fennel and cut the bulbs into quarters; fry them in olive oil till browned, add a tin of tomatoes and some mixed herbs. Either bake in a covered casserole in a medium oven till tender, or microwave (covered) until tender. You can add chicken breasts to make a meal.

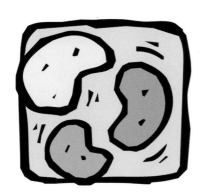

- ### Phyll's Leek And Butter Bean Crumble

Crumble

3oz soft margarine

5oz wholemeal flour
2oz chopped walnuts

Filling

1lb of cooked leeks
tin of butter beans drained
white sauce

a stick of celery, chopped
tin of tuna

Make the crumble by rubbing the margarine into the flour then adding the walnuts. Assemble the filling in an ovenproof dish and top with the crumble; cook at 190°C/375°F/Gas Mark 4 for 30 mins. Very filling: serve with French bread.

- ### Vegetarian Lasagne

white sauce or a tub of fresh three-cheese sauce
onion and clove of garlic, fried in butter *easy-cook lasagne*
tin of tomatoes *tin of ratatouille*
frozen spinach *mixed herbs*

In an ovenproof dish, alternate layers of lasagne with layers of mixed vegetables, herbs and onions and garlic till the ingredients are used up. Top with the white sauce and sprinkle with grated cheese, or use the tub of cheese sauce; bake in a medium oven for 45 minutes.

- ### Mushroom Quiche

parsley
8oz large mushrooms, chopped
butter

1oz grated cheddar cheese
3 eggs, beaten into 1/2pt milk
pastry

Sweat the mushrooms, parsley and butter together then cover and cook very gently for five minutes till the juices run out; then mix the mushrooms with the beaten eggs, milk and cheese. Line a flan dish with pastry and pour in the egg mixture; bake for about 30 minutes in a medium oven until slightly risen. Heats up OK in the microwave.

Puddings or Desserts

Blow the waistline: these will really make you popular with your friends and family.

- ### Danish Apple Cake

4oz butter
8oz self-raising flour
1 egg
½ teaspoonful ginger
flaked almonds

4oz sugar
2oz sultanas
2 tablespoons brown sugar
cinnamon
12oz cooking apples

Melt the butter and sugar in the microwave; add the ginger, flour and egg, and mix to a stiff paste. Grease an 8-9 inch tin with a removable base, and spread most of the mixture on the bottom, reserving a handful. Cut the apples into wedges and put on the base; cover with the sultanas, brown sugar and cinnamon. Roll four or five small balls out of the reserved base mixture and put these on top; sprinkle with almonds, then bake at 190°C/375°F/Gas Mark 5 for 40-45 minutes.

- ## Apples In Jackets

  cooking apples, cored and peeled *suet pastry as for Jam Roly Poly*
  sultanas or mincemeat

Stuff the hole in the middle of each apple with sultanas or mincemeat. Make rounds out of the pastry and put an apple on each one; press the suet round the apples with your hands, then roll each one in brown sugar. Bake in a hot oven for about 30 minutes or till crisp and brown.

- ## My Mum's Sherry Trifle

  a bought Swiss roll (jam sort)   *two glasses of sherry*
  a pack of frozen raspberries   *custard (home made or a packet)*
  whipped cream   *toasted almond flakes*

In a glass dish, soak the Swiss roll in sherry until it's soggy then add a layer of raspberries or other fruit. Cover with a layer of custard, cover that with a layer of whipped cream, then cover that with toasted almonds (either grilled lightly, or microwaved with a glass of water in the microwave with them).

- ## Jam Roly Poly (Like School Dinners)

  8oz self raising flour   *4oz shredded vegetable suet*
  1oz sugar   *jam*

Mix the flour, suet and sugar together with cold water until it forms a stiff paste. Knead this quickly and roll it into an oblong; spread the oblong with jam, leaving a small margin at the edge. Dampen the edge and roll up like a Swiss roll, pressing down the edges to seal them. Bake on a greased tray in a hot oven (200°C/400°F/Gas Mark 6) for 30-40 min; serve with custard.

Cookies and Cakes

These cookies and cakes are ideal for the quilt exhibition teas; you can make lots of money for your quilt group by selling them home-made cakes.

- ## Di's New Zealand Fruit Cake

  Tin of crushed pineapple, 15oz size   *1lb mixed fruit*
  1 teaspoonful bicarbonate of soda   *1 teaspoonful mixed spice*
  4oz butter   *4oz sugar*

Put all the ingredients in a saucepan and bring to the boil (until the mixture bubbles up). Turn off the heat and let the mixture cool, then add 8oz self-raising flour and two beaten eggs. Mix together well and put in large tin; bake for 1 hour in the top of oven at 200°C/400°F/Gas Mark 6; when the cake's brown enough, cover the top with foil until the end of the cooking time. Makes a very moist cake.

- ## Doro's Flapjacks

  6oz butter or margarine   *4oz demerara sugar*
  2 tablespoons syrup   *10oz porridge oats*

Melt the butter, sugar and margarine in a microwave, add the oats, then press the mixture into a tin and bake for 30-35 minutes until golden. When the baked mixture has cooled slightly, cut it into slices and leave to cool completely. My granddaughters love making these.

• Molly's Toffee Shortbread

Base	Toffee
6oz flour	*small tin of condensed milk*
2oz caster sugar	*4oz butter*
4oz margarine	*4oz caster sugar*

Cream the margarine and sugar for the base, add the flour, then press into a 6in square tin; bake for 20 minutes at 180°C/350°F/Gas Mark 4. Put all the ingredients for the toffee in a large pan, and boil gently for 4-5 minutes until thick and caramel-coloured. Cover the shortbread with the toffee, then cover the toffee with melted cooking chocolate. Cut into fingers when cold.

• Welsh Cakes

8oz self-raising flour	*2oz butter*
2oz lard	*3oz sugar*
2oz currants or sultanas	*1 egg, beaten*
2 tablespoons milk	

Rub the butter and lard into the flour; add the sugar and currants, then bind with the egg and milk to make a stiff paste. Roll out to ¼in thick, and cut into rounds with a 3in cutter or wine glass. Grease a frying pan and cook the cakes slowly for three minutes on each side until they are risen and brown. Toss in sugar and eat the same day. As you don't need an oven, these are fine for camping or caravan holidays!

• Dierdre's Ginger Shortbread

Base	Topping
4oz margarine	*1oz butter*
4oz self-raising flour	*4 tablespoons icing sugar*
2oz sugar	*3 teaspoonfuls syrup*
1 teaspoonful ginger	*1 teaspoonful ginger*

Cream the butter and sugar, add the flour and ginger, and press into a 6in square tin; bake for 20 minutes at Gas Mark 4. Meanwhile, make the topping by melting the ingredients slowly in a saucepan. Spread the topping on top of the cooked shortbread, let it harden and cool, then cut into squares.

• Baggy's Melting Moments

My grandma was always know as Baggy, which implies she was rather fat; in fact she was a slim Cumbrian lady who lived to be well in her 90s and always home baked.

5oz self raising flour	*4oz margarine or butter*
3oz caster sugar	*1 egg, beaten*
almond essence	*cornflakes*

Cream the margarine/butter and sugar till fluffy; add the flour and almond essence, and mix to a stiff paste with the beaten egg. Make into walnut-sized balls and roll in cornflakes; bake on a greased tray for 15 minutes at 180°C/350°F/Gas Mark 4. Cool on a wire rack

Sorry: you thought you'd bought a quilt book, not a cookery one! But I hope I've convinced you that you can cook and quilt – and have plenty of time to enjoy both.

Basic boring bits!

If you're an experienced quilter this bit isn't for you, but if you're a beginner this section explains how to do the basics.

ROTARY CUTTING

Rotary cutters speed up fabric cutting, and when accurate strips are essential, as with log cabin, they are invaluable. The cutters are available in large and small sizes, and you need a self-healing mat to cut on and a plastic see-through ruler. You can get mats with measurements marked on them, but I prefer a plain mat combined with a quilters' ruler marked with different measurements.

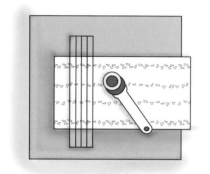

The grain of the fabric must be straight and the selvedge removed so that the fabric won't pull out of alignment while it's being cut. It is possible to cut many layers at once, but for beginners it's easier to do just two at a time. Place the fabric on the mat, put the ruler on top, hold the ruler firmly in place with your left hand, and cut with the cutter blade against the side of the ruler. Cut away from your body with an even movement.

Rotary cutters are very sharp and should be used with care. Always shut the blade after each cut, and keep the cutter well out of the way of small children. You can buy a gadget to re-sharpen the blades: these are useful to have in a quilt group so that people can sharpen the blades at each meeting. If you're keen, you'll find that there are many books devoted entirely to rotary-cut patterns.

MACHINE PIECING

This is obviously the quickest way of joining patchwork pieces. Make sure that you have a good relationship with your machine! Take time to read the instruction book and try out the different things it will do.

Most trouble for patchworkers seems to come with seam allowances. Instructions usually suggest a quarter inch (5mm) seam allowance. Some machines have a special patchwork foot which is marked out with notches at the correct intervals; if you don't have one just gauge it by the width of the foot, and stick to the same foot throughout your project. Another alternative is to measure the correct distance from your needle and stick a strip of masking tape onto the machine to use as a guide.

If you are contributing a block to a group quilt, this is when seam allowances really matter: if you have ever tried to *assemble* a group quilt you will know exactly what I mean!

HAND PIECING

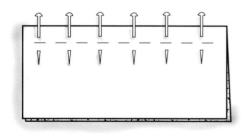

If you don't have a good relationship with your machine, or simply find hand-sewing a relaxing therapy as I do, you can piece accurately by hand. You will need to draw round your template on the back of each patch with a sharp pencil. Before sewing match the drawn lines and pin the pieces vertically to get an accurate join. Sew with running stitches, but with an occasional backstitch to keep it firm. When you get to an edge, leave the seam allowance unstitched so that it can be pressed to either side.

IRONING AND PRESSING

I find a travel iron very useful for small projects; it's also useful to have an iron nearby your machine when you are stitching. A small sleeve-ironing board is handy, or you can make a small board from the cardboard centre of a roll of fabric (smile at your local fabric shop assistant); this can be covered in some old flannelette sheet and is useful for taking to classes too.

It's usual to press the seams to the dark side of the work so that they don't show through a light fabric. Sometimes, though, with very thick fabrics you might need to press the seams out flat. Occasionally steam ironing can stretch the fabrics: I find that spraying the water from a plastic bottle means you get the dampness just where it's required. (I'm really mean and re-use household cleaner bottles for this.)

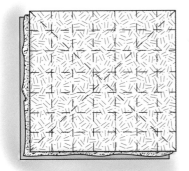

MAKING THE QUILT SANDWICH

This isn't a break for a snack! It's the way a quilt is put together. There are three layers: the top, which is usually made from pieced patches; the middle, which is the wadding (this can be polyester or cotton depending on the project or your preference); and the backing, which should be at least 4in (10cm) larger than the top. If your quilt is a bed quilt you will have to join the backing with a seam, or you could use sheeting which is very wide.

The secret of making the sandwich is to get it all flat and not puckered. Depending on the state of your knee joints you can either work on the floor or on a large table: the method is basically the same. OK, so most people don't have large tables and those who do might not want to lend them for tacking quilts on. Either buy a cheap decorating table which folds away and is useful for cutting, then pin half the quilt at a time, or ask the village or church hall if you can use their tables for an hour.

Tape the backing right side down if you're working on a wooden floor or a table: pin it if you're working on a carpet. Make sure that it's nice and taut, then place the wadding (batting, if you're American) on top, smoothing it out. If the wadding needs joining do so by butting the pieces together; don't make a seam, as that would show as a ridge. Place the quilt top right side up on top of the wadding and smooth it well.

If you are hand quilting, tack (baste) the layers together with even tacking stitches, first from corner to corner then from side to side at about 6in (15cm) intervals. This is a laborious job but worth taking time over as it makes the quilting easier and the back smooth if you do it well. There are also tack guns available these days, which shoot little plastic 'stitches' through the layers.

If you are machine quilting, secure the sandwich with safety pins, as the machine will get caught in tacking stitches. You'll need quite a few safety pins; sometimes these can be obtained from dry cleaners' very cheaply. To avoid hurting your fingers and getting blood on your quilt from your wounds you can close them by pushing the tips onto a teaspoon. When you remove the pins as you machine quilt leave them open; this saves time and effort the next time they are used.

BINDINGS AND BORDERS

This used to be a recurrent problem for me as I always seemed to end up with a wonky-edged quilt! I discovered that it works better if you measure a line through the centre of the quilt and cut each side to that measurement; the sides are then eased or stretched to the same dimension, making the final edge more accurate.

When you're binding a quilt, cut the binding strip twice as wide as required and iron it in half: when it's machined to the quilt edge as shown, it's simple to ease the folded edge over to the back ready for slipstitching in place. An even easier way of binding a quilt is to turn the backing fabric to the front: fold it over in a double fold and slipstitch it to the front. This does of course mean that your backing fabric has to be one that tones with the front of your quilt.

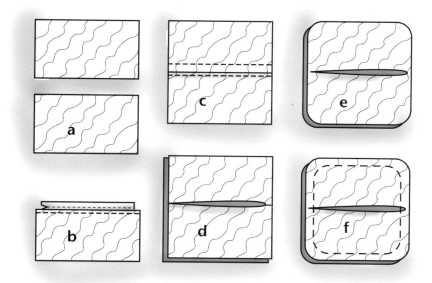

MAKING A CUSHION COVER

For a 12in (30cm) square cover

a Cut the fabric for the backing to 13x16in (33x41cm) and cut this piece in half to make two rectangles 13x8in (33x20.5cm). Fold under and iron a 1in (2.5cm) turning along one long edge of one rectangle, and a 2in (5cm) turning on the other piece.

b Position a 10in (25.5cm) zip under the narrower folded edge and stitch it into place using a zipper foot.

c Position the second piece so that the wider folded edge covers the zip, and machine this into place.

d Open the zip and place the cushion backing face down on the cushion front, right sides together; pin.

e Round the corners evenly; you can do this by drawing round a saucer rim if you're not confident of your curves.

f Machine round the edge and trim the corners. Putting the zip in first is much easier than trying to put it in after the cushion cover is stitched.

EMBROIDERY STITCHES FOR CRAZY PATCHWORK (below)

There are many different stitches that you can use for crazy patchwork, but these are the most common – and some of the most effective.

a Chain stitch
For each link in the chain, insert the needle where the thread emerges and loop the thread around the needle tip. Secure the final link of the chain with a small straight stitch.

b Lazy daisy or detached chain stitch
This stitch consists of individual chain stitches, each one caught down with a small straight stitch.

c French knots
Twist the thread two or three times round the needle, then pull it through to form a knot and take the needle to the back of the work.

d Fly stitch
Bring the needle out on the left of the work, then take it down at the right so that it emerges in a diagonal line as shown. Work a straight stitch vertically to secure each V-shape.

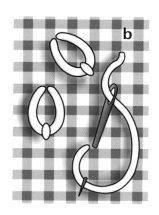
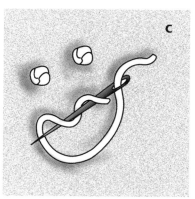

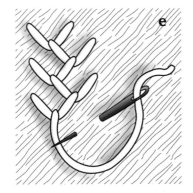

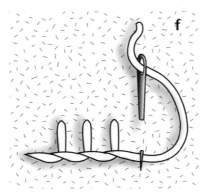

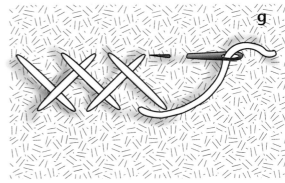

e Feather stitch
Take diagonal stitches alternately to the right and to the left of the stitching line, catching a loop of thread each time as shown.

f Blanket stitch
Create a series of right-angled stitches by putting the needle in vertically as shown. Secure the final loop with a small straight stitch.

g Herringbone stitch
Work from left to right, and take horizontal stitches alternately along the top and bottom of the stitching line to create a criss-cross pattern.

FLIP AND SEW
This method is used to cover a piece of foundation fabric with crazy or random piecing. You can trim the patches you add to size as you go, as shown, or leave them ragged at the top and bottom edges and trim them back once all the machining is complete.

a Lay a piece of fabric face down on the previous patch and stitch a straight seam through all layers by machine.

b Fold the new section to the right side and press: it's now ready to have a further patch added on its raw edge.

Acknowledgements

Thanks to:

John, for putting up with my mess for 37 years!

Gail and Christopher for their patience and expertise

Linda Tudor for use of our original pattern and method of cathedral window

The Surrey Advertiser, for use of the front cover photograph

Alan Masters and Peter Renn for some of the photographs

Zoë Stapleton for lending her quilt

Angela Besley, for use of a pattern from her book *Rose Windows for Quilters* (GMC Publications)

GRIDDED VILENE can be bought from some stockists, or direct from Dorothy Stapleton, 14 Windmill Drive, Leatherhead, Surrey KT22 8PW

BLUE-PRINTING CHEMICALS are available from: Silverprint Ltd, 12 Valentine Place, London SE1 8QH

Silverprint also stock the definitive book on the process: *Cyanotope, the history science and art of photographic printing in Prussian blue* by Mike Ware, published by The Science Museum.

The chemicals can also be bought by mail order from: Jim Cottrill, 10 The Triangle, Triggs Lane, Woking, Surrey GU21 1PP (tel 01483 772316)

READY-PREPARED BLUE-PRINTING FABRIC is available from: Home Crafts Direct, PO Box 39, Leicester LE1 9BU (tel 0116 251 3139; e-mail speccrafts.co.uk)

The fabric is in the photographic section; it comes in packs of thirty 150x150mm pieces, packed in a lightproof bag, and with instructions for use.